ENDORSEMENTS

Although angels have always been present in the affairs of humans, there seems to be an increase of their activity today. Through my understanding of *The Courts of Heaven* I have gained a new awareness and appreciation for this activity in the unseen realm. The scripture is clear that *we have come to an innumerable company of angels* (Heb. 12:22). This means that as New Testament believers we have been positioned in the spiritual dimension where angels and their activity occurs. I appreciate Kevin Zadai's insight into this realm. He helps us know how to recognize and move in agreement with this heavenly sphere. When we do, we gain supernatural impulse that allows God's breakthrough to impact our lives. This book helps us gain wisdom in partnering with angels and the place in the spirit they function from.

ROBERT HENDERSON
President of Global Reformers
Best-selling author of *Operating in The Courts of Heaven* and the *Court of Heaven* series.

Angelic activity in the earth has been increasing in great degrees over the last two decades. As a result, it is important to receive biblically based teaching on angels, their God-given assignments, and their interaction with man. Dr. Kevin Zadai, is a Bible scholar but has also had numerous spiritual encounters and life-transforming visitations in heaven. The *Agenda of Angels* is a must read. You will receive profound revelatory insights, sound biblical teaching, and Spirit-inspired impartation.

Dr. Patricia King
Founder Patricia King Ministries
Co-Founder XPmedia
www.patriciaking.com

The *Agenda of Angels* is the best manuscript I have read to date on the supernatural role that angels play in our lives and the Kingdom of God. The activity of the spirit realm is more real than the physical. And it is imperative as believers that we understand and recognize that it is our Kingdom inheritance to know of and to experience the realities of our eternal home now. Being a mother of a child who was a seer from a very young age, we came into a clear understanding that angels are always among us and always on assignment. It is beyond amazing that the Lord has assigned angels and angel armies to each of us, spheres of culture, cities, regions, and nations. This now message of Kevin Zadai will inspire you, teach you how to live and maneuver in a glory lifestyle with our King. Your spiritual senses will awaken and become aware to the supernatural realm and activity surrounding you and that angels are on assignment on your behalf now. Thank you, Kevin for this holy, anointed and empowering now message of the Lord.

Rebecca Greenwood
Cofounder
Christian Harvest International
Strategic Prayer Apostolic Network
Author of *Authority to Tread, Let Our Children Go,*
Defeating Strongholds of the Mind, and *Glory Warfare*

THE AGENDA OF ANGELS

THE AGENDA OF
ANGELS

WHAT THE HOLY ONES WANT YOU TO
KNOW ABOUT THE NEXT MOVE OF GOD

KEVIN L. ZADAI

DESTINY IMAGE® PUBLISHERS, INC.

P.O. Box 310, Shippensburg, PA 17257-0310

"Promoting Inspired Lives."

This book and all other Destiny Image and Destiny Image Fiction books are available at Christian bookstores and distributors worldwide.

Cover design by Eileen Rockwell

Interior design by Terry Clifton

For more information on foreign distributors, call 717-532-3040.

Reach us on the Internet: www.destinyimage.com.

ISBN 13 TP: 978-0-7684-4982-2

ISBN 13 eBook: 978-0-7684-4983-9

ISBN 13 HC: 978-0-7684-4985-3

ISBN 13 LP: 978-0-7684-4984-6

For Worldwide Distribution, Printed in the U.S.A.

1 2 3 4 5 6 7 8 / 23 22 21 20 19

DEDICATION

I dedicate this book to the Lord Jesus Christ. When I died during surgery and met with Jesus on the other side, He insisted that I return to life on the earth and that I help people with their destinies. Because of Jesus's love and concern for people, the Lord has actually chosen to send a person back from death to help everyone who will receive that help so that his or her destiny and purpose is secure in Him. I want You, Lord, to know that when You come to take me to be with You someday, it is my sincere hope that people remember not me, but the revelation of Jesus Christ that You have revealed through me. I want others to know that I am merely being obedient to Your heavenly calling and mission, which is to reveal Your plan for the fulfillment of the divine destiny for each of God's children.

ACKNOWLEDGMENTS

In addition to sharing my story with everyone through the books *Heavenly Visitation: A Guide to the Supernatural, Days of Heaven on Earth: A Guide to the Days Ahead, A Meeting Place with God, Your Hidden Destiny Revealed,* and *Praying from the Heavenly Realms: Supernatural Secrets to a Lifestyle of Answered Prayer* the Lord gave me a commission to produce this book, *The Agenda of Angels.* This book addresses some of the revelations concerning the areas that Jesus reviewed and revealed to me through the Word of God and by the Spirit of God during several visitations. I want to thank everyone who has encouraged me, assisted me, and prayed for me during the writing of this work, especially my spiritual parents, Dr. Jesse Duplantis and Dr. Cathy Duplantis. Special thanks to my wonderful wife Kathi for her love and dedication to the Lord and to me. Thank you, Sid Roth and staff, for your love of our supernatural Messiah, Jesus. Thank you, Dr. Janet Kline, for the wonderful job editing this book. Thank you, Destiny Image and staff, for your support of this project. Special thanks, as well, to all my friends who know about the agenda of angels and what they would want us to know about the next move of God's Spirit!

CONTENTS

FOREWORD

Before the development of radar and sonar, big ships faced a greater danger from icebergs. Sailors could see the very top of the iceberg, but it was only two percent of the total mass. Ninety-eight percent was hidden under the water. Because they couldn't see the threat, many ships were lost!

The same principle applies to believers in Yeshua. Ninety-eight percent of the action we face is in the invisible realm. Without angelic help to protect us from the icebergs (demons), we would face great peril! But if we cooperate with our angels and assign them by speaking directives of God out loud, they can help us steer clear of demonic attacks.

Kevin Zadai has been to Heaven and learned how to cooperate with the angels. As you feast on this heavenly instruction manual, your spiritual radar and sonar will become totally activated.

Why is this so important? Because Jesus is returning soon. How do I know? He told me three times in a dream: "I am coming soon! I am coming soon! I am coming soon!"

In these last days, there will be more angels and demons released on earth than at any time in history. Why? Because God's Greater Glory is about to be released suddenly—and soon! It has already started, but the degree of Glory that is coming will make all other moves of God's Spirit pale in comparison.

God has called you to be a front-line player in the last and greatest outpouring of His Spirit. As my friend Kevin likes to say, "The game is rigged in your favor!" This book will be your game changer.

SID ISRAEL ROTH
Host, *It's Supernatural!* TV show

INTRODUCTION

I often meet people who want to know all about my experience of being in the presence of Jesus. Being with Jesus on the other side of the veil that separates earth and Heaven is so extraordinary. I know that no one translated to that place would ever desire to come back to this world. But what if someone did come back? And what if he or she talked about being in the presence of Jesus?

When I received the mandate to write this book, I was given the contents as if I were in a briefing room with the angels. The environment of that military-style briefing that I encountered is reflected in this book. The angels that are assigned to us are a vast army with their commander, Jesus as their supreme authority.

The purpose of *The Agenda of Angels* is to share two very important truths I learned while in the presence of Jesus. These are the two essential truths—*value* and *security*.

The first truth that I learned is that God has placed great *value* upon every believer. God so values each believer that He wrote a book concerning the life of every Christian before God breathed that person into his or her mother's womb (see Ps. 139). Money does not exist in Heaven, but nevertheless a high price has been given for every person who ever has lived upon the earth. The Son of God paid the highest price of all for the spirits of men and women of the earth—the precious blood of Jesus. People are the most valuable asset to Heaven. Every person on earth can have eternal value. God's investment in every believer is an investment for each generation and also an investment for the eternal Kingdom of the Lord.

The second truth that I learned is that God has provided for every Christian's *security*. Jesus gives each Christian a great degree of *security* so that he or she can safely and effectively fulfill His will, as it is written in the book in Heaven for every believer. Every believer is safe in His care as He ushers each one into his or her destiny with Him. The mighty angels of God are in charge of this process. "God sends angels with special orders to protect you wherever you go, defending you from all harm" (Ps. 91:11 TPT).

These two truths, *value* and *security*, will give each believer *perfect love that will drive out all fear*. The purpose of *The Agenda of Angels* is to help each believer realize the fullness of God's love for him or her. First John 4:18 says, "There is no fear in love; but perfect love casts out fear, because fear involves torment. But he who fears has not been made perfect in love."

Jesus directed me to come back and speak to this generation for His divine purpose to tell the believers of this generation the truth. Jesus told me to reveal that I met with Him and that His desire for every Christian is that each one will know that the heavenly Father places great value upon the life of every Christian. *This present generation of Christians is being visited by God through angelic forces, but often believers do not fully discern this visitation of angels.* God has given His agenda into the hands of these faithful messengers of fire. The Commander of the Lord's army has briefed His special forces of angelic beings. Angels are ready to help every Christian to accomplish what is written in Heaven in this generation.

This generation of believers must now hear this particular message so they can fulfill what they must do for the Kingdom of the Lord. Subsequent generations of Christians need believers to have heeded this message. Christians are responsible for changing history, and the tool to change history is to present knowledge of *The Agenda of Angels.* Believers must return to their first love because the great and final move of the *glory of the Father* has already begun; it is His final act of filling the earth with His glory. Our Commander, Jesus Christ, wants every Christian upon the earth today to know that He is coming soon, and we Christians have our part to play in this final hour. Christians must cooperate with God's angels in His divine agenda before that great and glorious day of His return for His bride, the church. Christians must now know *The Agenda of Angels.*

KEVIN L. ZADAI, TH. D.

Chapter 1

THE VEIL OF SECRECY

Then Jacob awoke from his sleep and said, "Surely the
Lord is in this place, and I wasn't even aware of it!"
—GENESIS 28:16 NLT

As we get into this discussion about angels and their mission, I would like to first talk about the strategy of angels to operate in secrecy. Did you know that one of the most important aspects of any military operation is the veil of secrecy? It is to a military force's advantage to keep an element of surprise and invisibility, as much as is feasible, in any operation. Therefore, a large percentage of military operations are done in secret. The Most High God and His Kingdom operations function no differently—secret missions are vital to victory over the powers of darkness of this world.

Angels are considered to be "special forces" and have special assignments from the military branch of Heaven's Kingdom. "God sends angels with *special orders* to protect you wherever you go, defending you from all harm" (Ps. 91:11 TPT). It is amazing to me how much is going on around us about which we have absolutely no awareness or knowledge.

If the Lord gave anyone the ability to see into the spirit realm right now, it would humble that person when he or she sees the abundance of angelic activity. Being able to see into the realm of the spirit would actually help each person to stop worrying about anything that is going on in his or her life right now. We each have so much heavenly help around us that if we were cognizant of what is happening in the spirit realm, we would have much more confidence to trust that the Lord Himself is working on our behalf. The Lord has special plans for His people of destiny. The apostle Paul said, "'Eye has not seen, nor ear heard, nor have entered into the heart of man the things which *God has prepared for those who love Him.*' But God *has revealed* them to us through His Spirit. For the Spirit searches all things, yes, the deep things of God" (1 Cor. 2:9-10). Every Christian must establish a deep trust in our heavenly Father's love for us and His ability to accomplish all that concerns us. Each of us must have revelation concerning this truth before we can advance to success in every area of our lives. And God desires that our lives be successful, especially for His Kingdom.

THE LORD, BY HIS SPIRIT, IS SAYING TO YOU, "I
LOVE YOU WITH AN EVERLASTING LOVE. I, LONG
AGO, THOUGHT OF YOU AND BREATHED YOU
INTO YOUR MOTHER'S WOMB. I WROTE A BOOK
ABOUT YOUR DAYS BEFORE ONE DAY CAME TO
PASS! YOU ARE IN MY ARMS AND YOU ARE IN MY
PLANS. I WILL SEE TO IT THAT ALL MY PLANS FOR
YOU COME TO PASS. IF ONLY YOU WILL TRUST IN
ME! (SEE PSALM 139:16.)

UNVEILING THE OTHER REALM

In the spirit realm, the Lord is looking at the future of each Christian's life as if that future is His now! So why even worry or be concerned about the future? Our Father has planned out for each of His children something better than we could ever plan ourselves. There are things that are planned for every Christian that the angels know, but they are hidden from each of us for the moment. I am amazed at the intricacy of God's ways and how wonderful His thoughts are toward us. The psalmist wrote, "How precious also are Your thoughts to me, O God! How great is the sum of them! If I should count them, they would be more in number than the sand; when I awake, I am still with You" (Ps. 139:17-18).

I remember the first time I encountered an angel. This event happened in the spring of 1982. I did not pray to see an angel, nor did I particularly want to see an angel. Previously, I had sensed that angels had come into my room while I was praying. I was fully aware of the awesomeness of the presence of angels. And I was, as well, fully cognizant of the fear of the Lord that is upon His angels. I therefore had no desire to see an angel.

I remember seeking the Lord diligently at the time. I was asking God to help me deal with the workload that I was encountering with my college work. I was asking the Lord to help me because I had given up everything to attend this college, and I had to keep a certain grade point average to stay in the program. I was in a darkened room. It is important to note that the door to my dorm room was double-locked with a dead bolt.

I remember that while I was pacing the floor, I would momentarily open my eyes so I would not run into something in the room. I would approach the closed and double-locked door in my dorm room and then turn and walk the other way toward the windows. I did this continually for hours while I was praying in the spirit. I wanted the revelation that was in my spirit by the Holy Spirit to come up into my understanding. I really did not care how long it took for the truth to come up. I desperately needed to hear from God.

As I pressed on through in prayer, I started to spiritually sense freedom in the spirit all around me, and I also was spiritually sensing freedom within my entire being. There are times when a person prays that one can feel the warfare going on around one's being. Then, it can suddenly become obvious that a breakthrough has arrived. The very air clears and the person praying feels free, as if he or she is free to fully breathe once again. During this particular prayer time, suddenly, a huge surge of power hit me like a wave from the ocean. I fell to the floor in the middle of the room. I could not move, but somehow I was able to see the room with my spiritual eyes, not my physical eyes. It was as though I were suspended above my body. I could see a large angel standing in the doorway.

The door had physically opened! That was just not possible because, as I noted previously, that door was double-locked. I still was not mobilized as I watched the angel approach me. He bent down and grabbed me by the arm. He lifted me up, and I regained some of my strength. As I stood before him, I noticed his attire. From top to bottom, the angel wore a full Roman centurion's uniform. He was very tall. He may have been about nine or ten feet tall, and he perhaps weighed eight hundred pounds.

He spoke with such authority as he began to address me. He said that he had come on behalf of the Most High God. He said, "I have been sent from the presence of the Most High to tell you that you must separate yourself unto God. There are individuals whom you have befriended from whom you are to separate yourself. No longer spend time with these people, for not only are they not in the will of God, but these people are about to be judged."

While he was talking to me, I saw the individuals about whom he was speaking. The group consisted of a group of people about twelve in number who had befriended me. The angel started to talk to me about my calling, but then he was interrupted by the Holy Spirit. I could not hear what was being said to him by the Holy Spirit, but he held his hand up to motion for me to wait. He then told me that he was called immediately to another place. He asked me to go to the prayer room, which was down the hallway. He said that instead of his completing this message from the Most High God, the Holy Spirit would finish the message.

I objected to this situation. I was impressed with the awesomeness of this angel. He was standing within three feet of me. I wanted him to continue to talk to me. I was looking at him and was studying his armor, which was very intricate and beautiful. The power that came from this being was so amazing, and it was a natural reaction for me to want him to complete his message because no one would have wanted him to leave. I felt safe because of the authority that I sensed within this angel. He walked in such godly authority, and awareness of his authority within just made me boldly confident in the protection of God. I then said to the angel, "You are already here, so please, just finish the message."

At this, the angel became very stern with me, sterner than he previously had been. He said, "I said go to the prayer room, and do it now!" At this, the angel turned and pointed to the prayer room door, which was down the hallway. Then, the angel walked quickly down the hallway. As he walked away, he disappeared into thin air!

Six months after this experience with the angel, those twelve or so individuals were all expelled from college for misconduct. If I had not listened to the angel's warning from that evening, I would have been implicated as being part of their group, and I also would have been expelled. The angel was sent to help me understand a situation that I could not possibly have personally foreseen at the time that the angel revealed it to me. The angel also knew completely what would happen to these individuals in the next six months. God's foreknowledge had been revealed to me, and that angel was sent to warn me.

This situation reveals one purpose of angels, and that is that they are sent to help Christians do the will of God. I often wondered why the angel did not visit the others who were expelled to warn them about their misconduct. However, it seems as though he came to answer a prayer that I was praying in the spirit. I was praying in the spirit without knowing that through my prayers God would respond and would be sure to give me helpful information concerning my future. The information that the angel revealed assisted me in my life. This situation clearly demonstrates one reason why it is so vitally important to pray in the spirit as often as one possibly can. What I mean by praying in the spirit is also called praying in tongues, as spoken by the apostle Paul. It seems that praying in the spirit and angel activity are tied together. I have had several visitations of angels after praying in the spirit for long periods of time.

I have told this series of events from my life because I want Christians to understand that there is another spiritual world around us that we cannot always see. It is called the spirit realm, and it is the realm in which the Holy Spirit rules and reigns. The Holy Spirit is the master of the spirit realm.

The Holy Spirit is given to every Christian when he or she is born again. Second Corinthians 5:17 states that we are born again of the Spirit and that we are new creatures in Christ Jesus. "Old things have been passed away; behold all things have become new." So it is obvious that the same Holy Spirit who was in us at the new birth is the same Holy Spirit who baptizes us to overflowing and gives us a supernatural language called tongues.

PRAYING IN THE SPIRIT

The apostle Paul teaches us in First Corinthians 14 that when we pray in tongues, our spirit prays to God by the leading of the Holy Spirit. In Romans 8:26, the apostle Paul says that sometimes we do not know how to pray in our own intellect, but that the spirit prays according to the will God. When we pray in tongues, we often praise and worship God. He also mentions in First Corinthians 13 that we can pray in the tongues of men and the tongues of angels by the Spirit. The apostle Jude says that we should pray in the Holy Spirit, building ourselves up in the most holy of faith while staying in the love of God (see Jude 1:20).

Jesus told me in person that praying in the spirit causes us to move in the supernatural realm and that all of our prayers will be answered if we allow this process of praying in the spirit to happen in the flesh. So we are yielding our members, our bodies, by praying in tongues. And as Paul said in First Corinthians 14, when we pray in the spirit, our minds are unfruitful because we are praying out mysteries in the spirit. We may not understand what we are praying in our intellect, but our prayer is perfect, and God is able to respond easily to those perfect prayers. This coincides with First Corinthians 2 where Paul says:

> No one can know a person's thoughts except that person's own spirit, and no one can know God's thoughts except God's own Spirit. And we have received God's Spirit (not the world's spirit), so we can know the wonderful things God has freely given us. When we tell you these things, we do not use words that come from human wisdom. Instead, we speak words given to us by the Spirit, using the Spirit's words to explain spiritual truths. But people who aren't spiritual can't receive these truths from God's Spirit. It all sounds foolish to them and they can't understand it, for only those who are spiritual can understand what the Spirit means. Those who are spiritual can evaluate all things, but they themselves

cannot be evaluated by others. For, "Who can know the Lord's thoughts? Who knows enough to teach him?" But we understand these things, for we have the mind of Christ (1 Corinthians 2:11-16 NLT).

Therefore, we can begin to realize how important it is to be baptized in the Holy Spirit with the evidence of speaking in other tongues. This is clearly taught throughout the Bible and mentioned many times in the Book of Acts. We are believers after we receive salvation, and we are given the opportunity to be baptized with water, as well as to be baptized with the Holy Spirit. When the Holy Spirit would fall upon the people in the Book of Acts, they would begin speaking with other tongues. The act of speaking with other tongues was known, and still is known, as the initial evidence of the baptism of the Holy Spirit.

Satan fights the truth about speaking in tongues almost as much as any other subject. This is because it is of vital importance that every believer in these last days be filled with the Spirit and speak in other tongues as the Spirit gives utterance. Speaking in tongues exists so that the truth may be known and proclaimed through your mouth. In the Book of James, we clearly are told that the tongue is the member of the body that controls the whole body. So if the Spirit of God can get hold of a believer's tongue, then the Spirit of God can get hold of your life. This is why the Holy Spirit takes hold of your tongue when you are baptized with the Holy Spirit. Additionally, Romans 12:2-3 reveals that the soul is not saved through the born-again experience, but it must be transformed by the renewing of your mind by the Word of God. One's mind and emotions and will, those three parts of one's soul, must be renewed daily and be sanctified through our obedience to the Word.

The apostle James talks about the tongue being set on fire by the flames of hell and how through the Holy Spirit a person's tongue can be set on fire by the Holy Spirit. When one's tongue is set on fire by the Holy Spirit, one is speaking the truth in love and fulfilling the purpose for which the church was formed. Our bodies together as the Christian church represent Christ's body. The Holy Spirit is here to unify the body of Christ, the church, until we come into the fullness of Him who bought us. See the books of Ephesians and Colossians for clarification of these principles.

Therefore, anyone can understand how important it is to allow oneself to operate in the spirit world by yielding the members of the body to the Spirit. We yield our members by speaking other tongues. We also must walk in the spirit by submitting our flesh to the Spirit of God. By yielding to speak in tongues and by walking in the Spirit, we can begin to operate in the unseen realm where angels complete their missions. When we yield our mouths to speaking in tongues and our spirits to walking in the Word, we begin to live according to God's Word daily. As you speak the truth in a prayer that is sent from Heaven, which contains a perfect prayer, your spirit speaks forth truth. When your spirit speaks forth truth, the angels gather around you because they recognize that you have connected fully with their mission. Their mission is to see to it that you have what you need to walk out the plan and purpose of God for your life on this earth.

WORKING WITH ANGELS

As a Christian begins to use his or her members, especially the tongue, he or she will find himself or herself in the perfect will of God, working with angels! This might seem difficult to believe or even too good to be true. However, this is the kind of life God created us to live. And this is the very purpose for which angels were created—to expedite God's will for every Christian, to every Christian, and within every Christian! The writer of Hebrews explained the purpose of angels in our lives in this way:

> *Are they not all ministering spirits sent forth to minister for those who will inherit salvation? Therefore we must give the more earnest heed to the things we have heard, lest we drift away. For if the word spoken through angels proved steadfast, and every transgression and disobedience received a just reward, how shall we escape if we neglect **so great a salvation**, which at the first began to be spoken by the Lord, and was confirmed to us by those who heard Him, God also bearing witness both with signs and wonders, with various miracles, and gifts of the Holy Spirit, according to His own will?* (Hebrews 1:14–2:4)

Additionally, there are a number of truths revealed in the Book of Hebrews upon which we must concentrate. It is necessary to enter into a new mindset concerning the Kingdom of God, a mindset that understands these five truths concerning angelic beings. Your assignments on this earth are powerful and include working with angels. Here are the five truths that are essential for Christians to understand:

1. **Briefing one:** *Angels are sent forth* to minister for children of God.

2. Briefing two: *We must earnestly grasp* the truth that we have heard so that we do not drift away.

3. Briefing three: *What angels speak is steadfast.* They speak on behalf of God. Therefore, what angels speak is God's Word.

4. Briefing four: *Every transgression and disobedience will receive a just reward.* Therefore, how shall we escape if we in any way neglect our own salvation?

5. Briefing five: *The Lord speaks, and then what He has spoken is confirmed* by those who have heard it. God also confirms His Word with signs and wonders. To confirm His Word, God bears witness to what we have heard and spoken by *confirming the Word with signs wonders and various miracles and gifts of the Holy Spirit according to God's will.*

It is essential that we as Christians fully comprehend the fact that the unseen realm around all of us is more real than the realm we presently see and experience. The Spirit of God is the Spirit of truth. According to what Jesus has clearly explained, He leads us into all truth. If a person does a word study on the word *truth*, one will find that "truth" is translated as the word "reality." So it is correct to state that we have the Holy Spirit of reality coming into our life through the born-again experience. Then, we are filled to overflowing with God's Spirit through the experience of the baptism in the Holy Spirit. In Romans 8, God tells Christians how to yield to the Spirit and not to the flesh. This is essential so that we may walk in the Spirit and live our entire life through the leading of the Holy Spirit. By living a life filled with the Spirit of God, we will not fulfill the lust of the flesh. Once we, deep down in our hearts, become fully aware of this principle of living by His Spirit, we begin to know a new resource for victory. We then begin to realize that when we pray in the spirit, we pray out the truth. We know that the truth sets us free! And where the spirit of Lord is, there is freedom! He who has the Son is set free, free indeed.

So we can consider *briefing one,* working with angels, to be the understanding that angels have been sent to minister for us. But they will only minister that which is the will of God for our lives and for the Kingdom of God. So anything we do in the flesh nature is contrary to the Spirit of God. Anything we do in the flesh is also contrary to the will of God. According to the apostle Paul, we are to yield to the Spirit as children of God:

> *For those who live according to the flesh set their minds on the things of the flesh, but those who live according to the Spirit, the things of the Spirit. For to be carnally minded is death, but to be spiritually minded is life and peace. Because the carnal mind is enmity against God; for it is not subject to the law of God, nor indeed can be. **So then, those who are in the flesh cannot please God.** But you are not in the flesh but in the Spirit, if indeed the Spirit of God dwells in you. Now if anyone does not have the Spirit of Christ, he is not His. **And if Christ is in you, the body is dead because of sin, but the Spirit is life because of righteousness.** But if the Spirit of Him who raised Jesus from the dead dwells in you, He who raised Christ*

*from the dead will also give life to your mortal bodies through His Spirit who dwells in you. **Therefore, brethren, we are debtors—not to the flesh, to live according to the flesh. For if you live according to the flesh you will die; but if by the Spirit you put to death the deeds of the body, you will live. For as many as are led by the Spirit of God, these are sons of God*** (Romans 8:5-14).

Through these powerful words of the apostle Paul by the Holy Spirit we can see that the Holy Spirit is essential to our Christian lives. The Holy Spirit makes it possible for us to be able to live according to His impulses and His mindset and not to the impulses of the flesh. So angels are sent to minister for us only as we walk in the Spirit. Unfortunately, and far too often, angels' efforts are wasted on cleaning up the consequences of our disobedience. Angels then must work to keep us out of danger because of our lack of submission to the Holy Spirit. According to the writer of Hebrews, disobedience should not be tolerated. As we have already stated, there is a just reward for those who are disobedient or in rebellion to God's ways. Angels are not actually primarily sent to repair situations brought about by our own disobedience or rebellion. The real purpose of angels being sent into our lives is to work with us to help us in doing the Kingdom of God's work. Unfortunately, angels often have to waste time and effort trying to rectify situations in our lives that our rebellion creates. It is important to remember that we are children of God, and therefore we must realize that being led by the Spirit of God goes hand in hand with the fact that angels are sent to minister for us, the children of God, so that we are able to successfully complete our destiny for the Lord on this earth.

Briefing two has to do with staying focused and concentrated on the task at hand and not drifting from the assignment that God has entrusted to us. Angels are extremely focused and have certain orders they follow exactly, as specified by the Lord Jesus Christ. The Holy Spirit monitors the activities of angels to make certain that everything that we do coordinates fully with God's intent. As long as a child of God does the same thing—allowing the Spirit of God to rule one's inner man, carrying out God's word exactly as he or she has been asked—everything goes well. But if a Christian starts to drift away from the initial plan, entering sin and disobedience, then he or she can grieve the Holy Spirit. When someone grieves the Holy Spirit, angels cannot help someone to fulfill God's plan because the Christian is in disobedience and sin. Even the angel of the Lord in the Old Testament could be grieved. Angels had the right to judge the children of Israel when they moved in disobedience.

> *Behold, I send an Angel before you to keep you in the way and to bring you into the place which I have prepared. Beware of Him and obey His voice; do not provoke Him, for He will not pardon your transgressions; for My name is in Him. But if you indeed obey His voice and do all that I speak, then I will be an enemy to your enemies and an adversary to your adversaries. For My Angel will go before you and bring you in to the Amorites and the Hittites and the Perizzites and the Canaanites and the Hivites and the Jebusites; and I will cut them off. You shall not bow down to their gods, nor serve them, nor do according to their works; but you shall utterly overthrow them and completely break down their sacred pillars* (Exodus 23:20-24).

Clearly, the above Scripture passage reveals that God wants us to be obedient and walk with Him. The angel that was prepared to go with them was briefed on God's perfect will.

Although that angel was not always visible to the children of Israel, there was a hidden agenda—the angel was assigned to bring them into the land that God had prepared for them. We must always remember that though an angel is not always visible, God asks people to be aware of the angel, to obey his voice, and not to provoke him. Therefore, by this example we know that we are not to provoke angels. God even goes as far to say that we are not to disobey him because he will not pardon such transgressions for God's name was in him. The good thing about the angel in this situation was that God clearly stated that if you obey the angel, the Lord says that He will be an enemy to our enemies as well as an adversary to our adversaries. The angel was going to go before them and cut off their enemies. The Lord has promised that these angels will help to overthrow our enemies and completely break down the secret pillars that uphold our enemies. It is obvious that working with angels is something that really happens for those who choose to walk in the spirit. We must not faint or hold back from God's call and mission. We must be confident that angels are present to help us when we do what God has ordained us to do.

And now on to *briefing three*. This phase is focused on what angels speak. We need to be aware that angels speak for God. What angels speak is steadfast. Because they speak on behalf of God, their word is God's Word, and therefore it must be taken very seriously. If a Christian wants to have an angel serve him or her, and if a Christian wants to be included in the plans and purposes of God with angels, a person must take the words of angels seriously. Angel visitation is not to be taken lightly. Their participation with a person in the furtherance of the gospel and the Kingdom of God on the earth is a very serious matter to God as well as to His angels. Also, there is always a possibility that the angels who are assigned to a person at this present time in the angelic realm may be the very angels under that person's role in the next reign of Jesus Christ, in His millennial Kingdom. Therefore, it is important to develop a healthy relationship now with the angels who have come to help a person presently. It is crucial to respect their word and their actions, for to do so will be sowing into one's future relationship with them. It is quite possible that those very angels will be ministering with the same person for all eternity.

The *fourth briefing* of working with angels includes being responsible for heeding God's commands, as well as the commands of the angels that we receive. The Bible clearly says in Hebrews 2:2-3 that "every transgression and disobedience received a just reward, how shall we escape if we neglect so great a salvation." So it is quite clear that we are to pay attention to our own salvation, as well as to the harvest of others coming into the Kingdom. We must work with angels so that others may come in and enjoy salvation also. *Angels work behind the scenes* to minister for us. The ministry of angels includes bringing people into the Kingdom of God. They enjoy the salvation of human beings. Jesus talked about this in His ministry when He said, "Even so, I tell you, *there is joy among and in the presence of the angels of God* over one [especially] wicked person who repents (changes his mind for the better, heartily amending his ways, with abhorrence of his past sins) (Luke 15:10 AMPC).

It is important to remember not only to hear the Word of God but to receive and obey the Word of God. Angels are involved in speaking and doing the Word of God. It is an awesome thing to be included as a part of this last-day move of God. Let us not be like those who heard and did not heed. According to Scripture, we must know how important it is to obey angels. In the Book of Acts, we are told, "You who received the Law as it was ordained and set in order and delivered by angels, and [yet] you did not obey it!" (Acts 7:53 AMPC).

The *fifth and final briefing* according to the Book of Hebrews is that *the Lord speaks and then it is confirmed* by those who have heard it. When the Lord begins to confirm His Word with actions, working with angels then becomes evident and exciting. In the Book of Acts, it was evident that the Lord was with the believers because signs and wonders followed them. In fact, leadership of that day took note that they had been with Jesus (see Acts 4:13). We can say that one of the true manifestations of believers who preached the gospel was that signs and wonders followed them, confirming what was preached. It was said of the believers in Jesus' day, directly after His ascension, "So then, after the Lord had spoken to them, He was received up into heaven, and sat down at the right hand of God. And they went out and preached everywhere, the *Lord working with them and confirming the word through the accompanying signs.* Amen" (Mark 16:19-20). Behind the scenes, angels are part of many signs and wonders that occur when a person testifies of Jesus.

It is of great importance to grasp these five briefings in order to understand and begin to experience the world of angels operating under the veil of secrecy. They are fellow servants who have been sent to minister for us. They do not want to get credit for anything they do. Their desire is that Jesus and the Most High God get the glory from whatever they do for God.

*Now I, John, saw and heard these things. And when I heard and saw, I fell down to worship before the feet of the angel who showed me these things. Then he said to me, "See that you do not do that. **For I am your fellow servant, and of your brethren the prophets, and of those who keep the words of this book.** Worship God." And he said to me, "Do not seal the words of the prophecy of this book, for the time is at hand. He who is unjust, let him be unjust still; he who is filthy, let him be filthy still; he who is righteous, let him be righteous still; he who is holy, let him be holy still"* (Revelation 22:8-11).

TIME TO BE AWARE

Jacob the patriarch had this unseen, angelic realm unveiled to him one day as he lay down to rest. Jacob was about to find out that there was more going on around him than he perceived. He was part of God's plan for all of mankind. In fact, the Most High God expressed this plan to his grandfather, Abram, during a visitation in the same place. That place was Bethel. Years before, Abram experienced what is told in Genesis 12 and 13:

*Then the Lord appeared to Abram and said, "To your descendants I will give this land." And there he built an altar to the Lord, who had appeared to him. And he moved from there to the mountain east of Bethel, and he pitched his tent with Bethel on the west and Ai on the east; **there he built an altar to the Lord and called on the name of the Lord** (Genesis 12:7-8).*

*And he went on his journey from the South as far as Bethel, to the place where his tent had been at the beginning, between Bethel and Ai, to the place of the **altar which he had made there at first**. And there Abram called on the name of the Lord* (Genesis 13:3-4).

It is intriguing to realize that many have gone before us who have built altars and set themselves apart for the will of the Lord. And even though those altars may no longer be erected as they once were in this physical realm, the building of those altars caused something spiritual to happen that opened a gateway to Heaven. So Jacob grabbed one of the stones that was probably used by his grandfather, years before that time, for the altar. Jacob used that stone as a pillow. The anointing of God was in that rock because it had meaning to the Lord. That stone was once a piece of a secret altar built by a man (Abram) who believed God and saw Him who was invisible (see Heb. 11:27).

Jacob seems to have been in the same condition that many Christians find themselves today. We have forgotten the heritage that is in our *spiritual lineage as believers*. Therefore, although we may be wandering around in the desert looking for God's will, we must also be aware that when we sit down to rest, we actually may be using a secret rock that was used to open the heavenly realm. Every one of us is coming to the culminating point—that time when we are finished with our own works in the desert of our own lives. We can lay down to rest, and we may find ourselves at the gateway of Heaven. Angels are all around, and we must be ready to receive information concerning a secret mission:

Meanwhile, Jacob left Beersheba and traveled toward Haran. At sundown he arrived at a good place to set up camp and stopped there for the night. **Jacob found a stone to rest his head against** *and lay down to sleep. As he slept, he dreamed of a stairway that reached from the earth up to heaven. And he saw* **the angels of God going up and down the stairway.** *At the top of the stairway stood the Lord, and he said, "I am the Lord, the God of your grandfather Abraham, and the God of your father, Isaac. The ground you are lying on belongs to you. I am giving it to you and your descendants. Your descendants will be as numerous as the dust of the earth! They will spread out in all directions—to the west and the east, to the north and the south. And all the families of the earth will be blessed through you and your descendants. What's more, I am with you, and I will protect you wherever you go. One day I will bring you back to this land. I will not leave you until I have finished giving you everything I have promised you." Then Jacob awoke from his sleep and said,* **"Surely the Lord is in this place, and I wasn't even aware of it!" But he was also afraid and said, "What an awesome place this is! It is none other than the house of God, the very gateway to heaven!"** *The next morning Jacob got up very early. He took the stone he had rested his head against, and he set it upright as a memorial pillar. Then he poured olive oil over it. He named that place Bethel (which means "house of God"), although it was previously called Luz* (Genesis 28:10-19 NLT).

As a Christian continues to grow up in the nurture and admonition of the Lord (see Eph. 6:4 KJV), the revelation of the Holy Spirit should become the predominant factor in his or her life. The Spirit has the ability to open a person's eyes to see into His realm. The realm of the Spirit is the realm of reality. Our God is the God of angel armies that operate in this realm of reality. This realm is not visible to the naked eye. The prophet Micaiah saw this and proclaimed, "Then Micaiah continued, "Listen to what the Lord says! I saw the Lord sitting on his throne with *all the armies of heaven around him, on his right and on his left*" (1 Kings 22:19 NLT). I have found that even though angels do often operate behind the scenes in secret, we must constantly remind ourselves they and we serve Almighty God, who is also in this unseen realm. At this very moment in time, He is being worshiped by angel armies, armies who do His will!

> *Praise him, all his angels! Praise him, all the armies of heaven!* (Psalm 148:2 NLT)

Chapter 2

ABSOLUTE TRUTH

The sum total of all your words adds up to absolute truth,
and every one of your righteous decrees is everlasting.
—PSALM 119:160 TPT

One of the most profound characteristics I encountered when I was with Jesus in Heaven was the characteristic of absolute truth. This characteristic cannot be emphasized enough. One of the most difficult tasks that we have as believers in this generation is the implementation of this very subject into our thinking in daily life. If you want to interact with angels correctly and see the supernatural in your life, you must fully understand absolute truth.

The best way to start this process is to understand that one cannot separate God from truth. Everything that He does and says is based upon the truth that was established from the beginning. God is truth. When a person bases his or her life upon absolute truth, then that person is known as someone who is firmly established upon the solid Rock of God. If someone is known to have lied, then others will have trouble believing that person when he or she says something. Additionally, if someone does not keep his or her word, then that person is not reliable. Not keeping one's word causes mistrust in a relationship. Christians must understand the importance of telling the truth and keeping one's promises because the next move of God and the working of angels require Christians who are truthful. That move also requires that Christian do whatever they say they will do.

You see, in Heaven there is no difference between who someone is as a person and the word that one gives to someone else. The person and his or her word are considered to be one and the same. Why is this so? It is because everything that God says, He does. He does not say something and fail to perform it. Keeping His Word makes God totally reliable. In any relationship, when a person's word is kept and he or she follows through with that word, acting upon what was promise, it works to develop strong trust. That is a Hebrew way of thinking that also concerns the topic of faith. So in Heaven, God's Word is the foundation of the universe. His Word endures forever because He framed the world by His Word.

By faith we understand that the worlds were framed by the word of God, so that the things which are seen were not made of things which are visible (Hebrews 11:3).

The definition of *absolute truth* according to Noah Webster is the following:

Absolute (adjective)

1. Literally, in a general sense, free, independent of anything extraneous. Hence,

2. Complete in itself; positive; as an absolute declaration.

3. Unconditional, as an absolute promise.

4. Existing independent of any other cause, as God is absolute.

5. Unlimited by extraneous power or control, as an absolute government or prince.

6. Not relative, as absolute space.

Truth (noun)

1. Conformity to fact or reality; exact accordance with that which is, or has been, or shall be. The truth of history constitutes its whole value. We rely on the truth of the scriptural prophecies.

My mouth shall speak truth. Proverbs 8:7.

Sanctify them through thy truth; thy word is truth. John 17:17.

2. True state of facts or things. The duty of a court of justice is to discover the truth. Witnesses are sworn

to declare the truth the whole truth and nothing but
the truth.[1]

These word studies reflect the fact that God Himself is the
author of truth. He is able to consistently enforce and preserve that
truth for all eternity. No one can amend what God has already
established in Heaven. God has the final word on everything in
His Kingdom.

THERE ARE NO SUGGESTION BOXES IN HEAVEN

God Almighty is eternal, meaning that He has always existed
and always will exist in a realm that has no time, no distance, nor
any other limitations. The prophet Isaiah said, "For thus says the
High and Lofty One who inhabits eternity, whose name is Holy:
'I dwell in the high and holy place, with him who has a contrite
and humble spirit, to revive the spirit of the humble, and to revive
the heart of the contrite ones'" (Isa. 57:15).

In order to grasp the concepts that concern God's existence
before time, we need to have our minds transformed so that we
can begin to understand what eternity encompasses. This requires
us to rely fully on the Holy Spirit, the *Revealer of Truth*. After a
Christian asks the Holy Spirit to come and reveal the truth, we
must reinforce the truth by the renewing of our minds (see Rom.
12:2). After someone permits this process to bring him or her to
maturity as a Christian, then the person will begin to understand
the personality of God and His plan and purpose for humanity. If
a Christian is planning to work with angels, it is essential for that
person to understand the personality of God. God's way of doing
things is not based upon man's opinion or suggestions. The Lord

God Almighty has been established in truth long before any person ever existed. The angels were created before man; they do not have an opinion. Angels were created to carry out the Lord's will. The psalmist says, "Bless the Lord, you His angels, who excel in strength, who do His word, heeding the voice of His word" (Ps. 103:20).

Angels understand eternity and *absolute truth*. Everything that God says is permanent so *there are no suggestion boxes in heaven*. The fear of the Lord will help Christians to accept the will of God. Additionally, what God has already established as truth will also help Christians to accept the will of God. Knowing the fear of the Lord brings humility. Having the fear of the Lord helps a Christian to more fully comprehend that the Lord God is the All-Knowing One.

When I have encountered angels, they were simply relaying the absolute truth of God to me. What the angels shared was definitely not up for discussion. There was no place for expression of my opinion concerning why God sent them. *Angels cannot be our friends unless we are first friends of God*. They only carry out orders and are not emotionally attached to us as they are to the Lord. Therefore, angels will never agree with us if our statements do not agree with the Lord. Remember that God told Moses in the Book of Exodus, "Behold, I send an Angel before you to keep you in the way and to bring you into the place which I have prepared. Beware of Him and obey His voice; *do not provoke Him, for He will not pardon your transgressions; for My name is in Him.* But if you indeed obey His voice and do all that I speak, then I will be an enemy to your enemies and an adversary to your adversaries" (Exod. 23:20-22). The message to the church and all believers concerning angels is this:

Do not grieve or provoke your angels!

Truth Is Foundational

Righteousness and justice are the foundation of your throne. Unfailing love and truth walk before you as attendants (Psalm 89:14 NLT).

The Lord has laid His foundation of truth, and that truth began at His throne. The very layers of God's throne are righteousness and justice, according to the psalmist. The Lord judges justly because the seat of His authority contains a layer of justice within that seat of authority. He rules rightly because His throne has a layer of righteousness that is found within that very throne. When God speaks, the foundation that He has laid gives Him power and authority.

The power and the authority that comes from God Almighty's voice as He sits on His throne is power and authority that transcends human imagination. When His voice rumbles, the fear of the Lord becomes completely present in that place. Psalm 89 refers to attendants that walk before God's throne. Those attendants are named *unfailing love* and *truth*. The throne is also where the holy angels stand as well. They surround the throne and behold our heavenly Father. These mighty messengers hear and obey the voice of the Lord. These angels do His bidding.

The Lord has established His throne in heaven, and His kingdom rules over all. Bless the Lord, you His angels, who excel in strength, who do His word, heeding the voice of His word. Bless the Lord, all you His hosts, you ministers of His, who do His pleasure. Bless the Lord, all His works, in all places of His dominion. Bless the Lord, O my soul! (Psalm 103:19-22)

There are a number of truths revealed in these verses of Psalm 103 that a Christian must realize are essential to begin to comprehend God's power and authority, as well as essential to the understanding of the purpose for which angels exist. I sense we must concentrate on the Foundation of absolute truth. It is necessary to enter into these mindsets concerning the Kingdom of God. Your assignments on this earth are powerful and include working with angels. Here are four very important briefings:

1. **Briefing one: The Lord has established His throne in Heaven.**

2. **Briefing two: His Kingdom rules over all.**

3. **Briefing three: His angels do three amazing things for God Almighty. Angels will always do the following things:**

   - Excel in strength.

   - Do His Word.

   - Heed the voice of His Word.

4. **Briefing four: All of His angelic hosts are His ministers, and they always will do the following things:**

   - Do God's pleasure.

   - Preside over all of His works.

   - Be present in all places of His dominion.

We will start with *briefing one* concerning the fact that the Lord has established His throne in Heaven. God is from a timeless realm, and He therefore has no limitations. God's limitless potential is unlike the limitations of human beings. It is hard to understand the fact that the Lord has existed always and will continue to exist forever. Due to His everlasting existence, the Lord's throne has always been, and will always be, the seat of power for all creation. The Father, the Son, and the Holy Spirit were all together in a preexistent state long before man was ever created. In fact, the holy angels were created before mankind. The Almighty is quoted in Job as asking:

> *Where were you when I laid the foundations of the earth? Tell Me, if you have understanding. Who determined its measurements? Surely you know! Or who stretched the line upon it? To what were its foundations fastened? Or who laid its cornerstone, when the **morning stars** sang together, and all the **sons of God** [angels] shouted for joy?* (Job 38:4-7)

We must realize that the God of the universe has always existed. Angels in Heaven will be dispatched to serve us for this last move of His Spirit on the earth. Angels were created before we were created. They are part of the pre-existing Kingdom of God. To fully comprehend the power that angels have at their beck and call, one must accept the fact that God has eternal existence. And in His pre-existence, He established a throne. From that throne, He rules the universe with authority. Mighty angels were also created before we were created. Their purpose has always been to fulfill God's plans. The Lord establishes His plans from His throne, and His throne is fully established in Heaven.

As we continue with *briefing two*, we must realize these facts: God was preexistent, and the Lord rules over all that He has created. *His Kingdom rules over all creation.* The angels understand the authority that God has within all of creation because they were created before we were created. No one, as well as no force, will ever be able to create another authority that could overtake God or place Him out of the seat of His power. Angels have been sent throughout the universe to enforce God's rule over creation, and they will continue until what the apostle Paul spoke of in the Book of Romans comes to pass:

> *For I consider that the sufferings of this present time are not worthy to be compared with the glory which shall be revealed in us. For the earnest expectation of* the **creation eagerly waits for the revealing of the sons of God** (Romans 8:18-19).

We are chosen to rule and reign with Him in the next life, as well as within this present life. Paul refers to Christians as the "sons of God." As Christians, we walk in the Spirit and do not fulfill the lusts of the flesh. "For as many as are led by the Spirit of God, these are sons of God" (Rom. 8:14). So angels, as fellow servants, implement the Kingdom of God along with Christians.

We are coming into a very special time in the days ahead. Angels are coming alongside Christians to start a huge domino effect in the Spirit. Revelation 19:10 states this information:

> *At this I fell facedown at the angel's feet to worship him, but he stopped me and said, "Don't do this!* **For I am only a fellow servant with you** *and one of your brothers and sisters who cling to what Jesus testifies.*

Worship God. The testimony of Jesus is the spirit of prophecy" (TPT).

Be prepared, because many Christians will be activated in this hour; we will become part of the "domino effect of Heaven." This "domino effect" alludes to this situation: Christians will begin to systematically influence others as those Christians have been influenced by Heaven. This heavenly influence will additionally include the ministry of angels to Christians. This procedure is a Kingdom secret.

Briefing three teaches us that *His angels do three amazing things for God Almighty.* Number one is that angels *always excel in strength.* They are energized by the power that comes from the throne of God. We must comprehend two entirely different types of spiritual power. We must understand both definitions of power in order to gain understanding concerning angels and their mission to assist us in completing our destiny for the Lord. These two types of power are explained below.

POWER

1. ἐξουσία—exousia (G1849)

*But those who embraced him and took hold of his name were given **authority** to become the children of God! He was not born by the joining of human parents or from natural means, or by a man's desire, but he was born of God* (John 1:12-13 TPT).

Strong's dictionary definition: from G1832 (in the sense of ability); privilege, i.e. (subjectively) force, capacity, competency, freedom, or (objectively) mastery (concretely, magistrate, superhuman, potentate, token of control), delegated influence—authority, jurisdiction, liberty, power, right, strength.

AV (103)—power 69, authority 29, right 2, liberty 1, jurisdiction 1, strength 1.

- Power of choice, liberty of doing as one pleases.

- Leave or permission.

- Physical and mental power the ability or strength with which one is endued, which he either possesses or exercises.

- The power of authority (influence) and of right (privilege); the power of rule or government (the power of him whose will and commands must be submitted to by others and obeyed).

2. δύναμις—dynamis (G1411)

*But you shall receive **power** when the Holy Spirit has come upon you; and you shall be witnesses to Me in Jerusalem, and in all Judea and Samaria, and to the end of the earth* (Acts 1:8).

Strong's dictionary definition: from G1410; force (literally or figuratively); specially, miraculous power (usually by implication, a miracle itself)—ability, abundance, meaning, might (-ily, -y, -y deed), (worker of) miracle (-s), power, strength, violence, mighty (wonderful) work.

AV (120)—power 77, mighty work 11, strength 7, miracle 7, might 4, virtue 3, mighty 2, misc 9.

- Strength power, ability, inherent power, power residing in a thing by virtue of its nature, or which a person or thing exerts and puts forth.

- Power for performing miracles. Moral power and excellence of soul.

- The power and influence which belong to riches and wealth.

- Power and resources arising from numbers.

- Power consisting in or resting upon armies, forces, hosts.

Angels always *do His Word*. This is part of the revelation of *absolute power* in the Kingdom of God. They are faithful servants who want to do His will. God's Word is His will. We know Him by His Word, which is written for us, as well as incarnate through the person of Jesus Christ.

> *In the beginning the **Word** already existed. The **Word** was with God, and the **Word** was God. He existed in the beginning with God. God created everything through him and nothing was created except through him. The **Word** gave life to everything that was created, and his life brought light to everyone. The light shines in the darkness, and the darkness can never extinguish it* (John 1:1-5 NLT).

The Word is a person named Jesus, and because of this spiritual truth the angels *heed the voice of His Word*. One cannot ever separate God from His Word because they are one and the same. Do you have any questions of the authority of what God says? If you answered, "Yes," then you are questioning God's very existence and authority. Angels are convinced of this truth. Absolute truth is based upon integrity that what God says He is fully able to accomplish. This principle is the foundation of the Kingdom of God. Angels obey because of God's integrity toward all He has created. When He speaks, whatever He has spoken will come to pass. "So will My word be which goes out of My mouth; it will not return to Me void (useless, without result), without *accomplishing* what I desire, and without succeeding in the matter for which I sent it" (Isa. 55:11 AMP).

Briefing four is the final instruction on this matter of *absolute truth. Christians will have to accept this final instruction* in order to participate in this end-time move of the Spirit in the Kingdom of God. *All of His angelic hosts are His ministers!* What is a minister? *Strong's Concordance* has the answer for us.

διακονία—*minister (G1248)*

Strong's dictionary definition: from G1249; attendance (as a servant, etc.); figuratively (eleemosynary) aid, (official) service (especially of the Christian teacher, or technically of the diaconate)—(ad-) minister (-ing, -tration, -try), office, relief, service (-ing).

AV (34)—ministry 16, ministration 6, ministering 3, misc 9.

Service, ministering, esp. of those who execute the commands of others.

These angelic ministers have certain characteristics. First, God commands angels to perform tasks, and they must do these tasks flawlessly for God. These angelic ministers *do His pleasure.* Angels want to please God and carry out His desires. These desires are God's heart on any given matter. Remember, God's desires are based on absolute truth, and absolute truth will always produce *absolute rule*. The angels then carry out special missions based on God's Kingdom business. We are part of these plans as His children. In these last days, God desires to see the harvest to come in.

> *If then God so clothes the grass, which today is in the field and tomorrow is thrown into the oven, how much more will He clothe you, O you of little faith? And do not seek what you should eat or what you should drink, nor have an anxious mind. For all these things the nations of the world seek after, and your Father knows that you need these things. But seek the kingdom of God, and all these things shall be added to you. Do not fear, little flock, for **it is your Father's good pleasure to give you the kingdom*** (Luke 12:28-32).

Second, *angels are over all His works*. They implement and maintain God's will, and His will is His heart for all creation. No angel questions the authority and rule of God. Angels were created for the purpose of oversight and implementation of what God commands. We can depend on the angels to execute missions in the heavenly realms and implement them on our behalf in the physical, earthy realm.

Third, angels are over *all places of His dominion. Dominion* is a strong word that has to do with driving the enemies of God out of His domain and maintaining secure borders. In Psalm 91, the Lord says:

> *God sends angels with special orders to protect you wherever you go, defending you from all harm. If you walk into a trap, they'll be there for you and keep you*

from stumbling. You'll even walk unharmed among the fiercest powers of darkness, trampling every one of them beneath your feet! (Psalm 91:11-13 TPT)

So that if I am delayed, you will know how people must conduct themselves in the household of God. **This is the church of the living God, which is the pillar and foundation of the truth** (1 Timothy 3:15 NLT).

THE THRONE

God's throne room is an awesome place. References in the Bible can help us to gather enough information to establish a clear picture of the appearance of the throne room. A throne symbolically represents a seat of authority. Everything that is in a king's throne room represents the kingdom in which he reigns. We see this in the Book of Isaiah.

It was in the year King Uzziah died that I saw the Lord. He was sitting on a lofty throne, and the train of his robe filled the Temple. Attending him were mighty seraphim, each having six wings. With two wings they covered their faces, with two they covered their feet, and with two they flew. They were calling out to each other, "Holy, holy, holy is the Lord of Heaven's Armies! The whole earth is filled with his glory!" Their voices shook the Temple to its foundations, and the entire building was filled with smoke. Then I said, "It's all over! I am doomed, for I am a sinful man. I have filthy lips, and I live among a people with filthy lips. Yet I have seen the King, the Lord of Heaven's Armies." Then one of

*the seraphim flew to me with a burning coal he had
taken from the altar with a pair of tongs. He touched
my lips with it and said, "See, this coal has touched
your lips. Now your guilt is removed, and your sins
are forgiven* (Isaiah 6:1-7 NLT).

We need to meditate upon this passage of Scripture as often as
possible. Meditating upon these verses will help to transform our
minds and our thinking. This activity in the throne room of God
occurs constantly. Angels are continually worshiping God and
attending to Him. Almighty God is in authority, and the throne
room represents His full authority. Nothing in this throne room
will ever change because God has established His Kingdom forever. As we just mentioned in the previous verses from Isaiah:

*Attending him were mighty seraphim. They were
calling out to each other, "Holy, holy, holy is the Lord
of Heaven's Armies! The whole earth is filled with his
glory!" Their voices shook the Temple to its foundations, and the entire building was filled with smoke.*

The Lord has laid a foundation for His Kingdom, and this
foundation is truth. It is absolute and endures forever. Just like
the psalmist says, "For the Lord is good; His mercy is everlasting,
and His truth endures to all generations" (Ps. 100:5). Even God's
throne is built on truth and righteousness. God sits on the seat
of His power over the universe. He is ruling and reigning over
His creation. This earth was taken from man, but we now have a
redemption process that began with Jesus. It began with His life,
death, burial, resurrection, and ascension. It will be culminated
at the end of the age when we have brought in the harvest. As we
bring in that harvest, the angels will be assisting us.

> *Righteousness and justice are the foundation of your throne. Unfailing love and truth walk before you as attendants* (Psalm 89:14 NLT).

The attendants that are around His throne are love and truth. This is where the angels stand as well!

> *All heaven will praise your great wonders, Lord; myriads of angels will praise you for your faithfulness. For who in all of heaven can compare with the Lord? What mightiest angel is anything like the Lord? The highest angelic powers stand in awe of God.* **He is far more awesome than all who surround his throne.** *O Lord God of Heaven's Armies! Where is there anyone as mighty as you, O Lord? You are entirely faithful* (Psalm 89:5-8 NLT).

As Christians, we must permit these truths concerning the scenario at the throne room to renew our minds. We can constantly renew our minds if we follow what Paul teaches in the Book of Romans. When we will renew our minds in such a way, we enter into the realm that encompasses angels. We will then be able to have their help in the missions that we must accomplish.

> *I beseech you therefore, brethren, by the mercies of God, that you present your bodies a living sacrifice, holy, acceptable to God, which is your reasonable service. And do not be conformed to this world, but be transformed by the renewing of your mind, that you may prove what is that good and acceptable and perfect will of God* (Romans 12:1-2).

Angels have a great understanding of God's personality and authority. They have learned about His personality and authority through observation of the Lord as well as interaction with God Himself. The angels constantly observe not only the display of God's mighty power but His beauty. If we meditate upon all of the Bible passages that describe God's throne and His character, we also will begin to understand what the angels see all the time.

> *He is the Rock, His work is perfect; for all His ways are justice, a God of truth and without injustice; righteous and upright is He* (Deuteronomy 32:4).

NEW COVENANT TRUTH

We need to discern that we are being visited by God's Spirit. Our present time reveals the revelation of God's Son, Jesus. He is the exact representation of the Father God in His glory.

> *Throughout our history God has spoken to our ancestors by his prophets in many different ways. The revelation he gave them was only a fragment at a time, building one truth upon another. But to us living in these last days, God now speaks to us openly in the language of a Son, the appointed Heir of everything, for through him God created the panorama of all things and all time. The Son is the dazzling radiance of God's splendor, the exact expression of God's true nature—his mirror image! He holds the universe together and expands it by the mighty power of his spoken word. He accomplished for us the complete cleansing of sins, and then took his seat on the highest throne at the right hand of the majestic One. He is*

infinitely greater than angels, for he inherited a rank and a Name far greater than theirs (Hebrews 1:1-4 TPT).

We are beginning to encounter, at this time, a full-out revelation of Jesus to the church. This is the same Holy Spirit, the One poured out upon the people in the Upper Room on the day of Pentecost. We are no longer kept from the revelation concerning what God is doing in our present time. The apostle Paul prayed that our eyes would be open to see into the realms of the Spirit.

I pray that the Father of glory, the God of our Lord Jesus Christ, would impart to you the riches of the Spirit of wisdom and the Spirit of revelation to know him through your deepening intimacy with him. I pray that the light of God will illuminate the eyes of your imagination, flooding you with light, until you experience the full revelation of the hope of his call-ing—that is, the wealth of God's glorious inheritances that he finds in us, his holy ones! (Ephesians 1:17-18 TPT)

Truth is being revealed by the Spirit of revelation. Right now, you are receiving revelation by His Spirit of truth about your des-tiny. Do we as Christians not realize that we have been brought into the Kingdom for this time and the angels have helped to position us to fulfill divine purposes? "And who knows whether you have attained royalty for such a time as this [and for this very purpose]?" (Esther 4:14 AMP).

"ALL IS WELL," SAYS THE LORD. "YOU ARE MY PRECIOUS CHILD AND ARE BEING GROOMED IN MY PRESENCE AND SHARE IN THE LOVE OF OUR FATHER. NO NEED TO BE BOTHERED BY INAC-TIVITY. YOU ARE IN MY PLAN AND THE ANGELS HAVE THEIR ORDERS CONCERNING YOU. YOU WILL SUCCEED AS YOU YIELD YOUR WILL OVER TO ME."

The revelation throughout all of history, especially through Moses and the prophets, brings our understanding of truth to a certain degree of revelation. When Jesus, the appointed Heir of everything, came, He revealed truth. Additionally, through His authority God maintains the universe. The universe expands by the authority of His own spoken word. Jesus redeemed us. He bought us back with His blood. He reconciled us to the Father God. He walked into Heaven and was seated on the highest place of authority. Jesus sits upon a throne at the right hand of the Most High. The angels worship Him as they stand in rank around the throne.

Remember how the Lord revealed Himself to Moses? He clearly proclaimed who He is in all His glory as He passed by Moses on the mountain called Sinai.

Now the Lord descended in the cloud and stood with him there, and proclaimed the name of the Lord. And the Lord passed before him and proclaimed,

*"The Lord, the Lord God, merciful and gracious, long-suffering, and **abounding in goodness and truth**, keeping mercy for thousands, forgiving iniquity and transgression and sin, by no means clearing the guilty, visiting the iniquity of the fathers upon the children and the children's children to the third and the fourth generation"* (Exodus 34:5-7).

Now, Jesus is the center of attention in Heaven. And, as we look to the Holy Spirit for revelation, we look to Him. In the gospel of John it states, "I am the Way, *I am the Truth*, and I am the Life. No one comes next to the Father except through union with me. To know me is to know my Father too" (John 14:6 TPT). What we have in Jesus is far greater than what Moses received. Jesus became flesh and blood and walked among us. The incarnation of Christ helps us to know the Father in a greater measure. Our understanding is increased through what we have seen and heard.

*And the Word became flesh and dwelt among us, and we beheld His glory, the glory as of the only begotten of the Father, full of grace and truth. John bore witness of Him and cried out, saying, "This was He of whom I said, 'He who comes after me is preferred before me, for He was before me.'" And of His fullness we have all received, and grace for grace. For the law was given through Moses, but grace and **truth** came through Jesus Christ. No one has seen God at any time. The only begotten Son, who is in the bosom of the Father, He has declared Him* (John 1:14-18).

The angels have the privilege of working for God, and for us as well, in this end-time harvest. Jesus is the central figure of this revelation of salvation. The angels see the face of our heavenly Father continually. Jesus clearly warns those who would even touch us in this work that we have been called to do.

*Take heed that ye despise not one of these little ones; for I say unto you, That in heaven **their angels do always behold the face of my Father which is in heaven*** (Matthew 18:10 KJV).

THE WORD OF TRUTH

Jesus continually emphasized the fact that the words that He spoke were what the Father was telling Him to speak. He also continually reminded everyone that His words were spirit and they were life. Jesus was taking the heart of the Father from the spirit realm and making God known in the physical realm. Jesus was able to make God known in the physical realm by speaking the Father's words, by acting those words out, and by healing humanity. Manifestation of the truth is very important when we speak about truth. In fact, we must not just believe, but we must speak what we believe also. The angels are activated by our words. So when we speak the truth, we are coordinating our words with the words that are being spoken in Heaven.

The angels that are assigned to us will implement our words when they are spoken by the Spirit of God. God speaks those words forth because He is the Spirit of truth. Manifestation of the truth will come. The angels are on duty at this very moment to make manifestation of the Word of God and truth come forth into your life. The Son of God speaks, and we are set free!

*Then Jesus said to those Jews who believed Him, "If you abide in **My word**, you are My disciples indeed. And you shall know the **truth**, and the **truth** shall make you free." They answered Him, "We are Abraham's descendants, and have never been in bondage to anyone. How can You say, 'You will be made free'?" Jesus answered them, "Most assuredly, I say to you, whoever commits sin is a slave of sin. And a slave does not abide in the house forever, but a son abides forever. Therefore if the Son makes you free, you shall be free indeed"* (John 8:31-36).

THE TRUTH IS IGNITED RIGHT NOW, AS THE WORD OF THE LORD FORMS INSIDE OF YOU AND CREATES A FIRE. SPEAK THE TRUTH OF THE LORD JESUS CHRIST FROM THAT FIRE WITHIN, AND WATCH WHAT HAPPENS. THE ANGELS WILL BEGIN TO MINISTER FOR YOU AT THIS VERY HOUR!

THE SPIRIT OF TRUTH

*But the hour is coming, and now is, when the true worshipers will worship the Father in **spirit and truth**; for the Father is seeking such to worship Him. God is*

Spirit, and those who worship Him must worship in
spirit and truth (John 4:23-24).

Another aspect of *absolute truth* in the earth is this: the Holy Spirit was sent to us. Through this mighty member of the Trinity, we can experience the power, presence, and authority of God Himself. One of the most important things to know about the Holy Spirit is that He is the Spirit of truth. Jesus announced that the Holy Spirit was coming:

> *If you love Me, keep My commandments. And I will pray the Father, and He will give you another Helper, that He may abide with you forever—**the Spirit of truth**, whom the world cannot receive, because it neither sees Him nor knows Him; but you know Him, for He dwells with you and will be in you. I will not leave you orphans; I will come to you* (John 14:15-18).

We now have the Holy Spirit inside of us, and He is wanting to speak out and testify of God. So when we pray in the Spirit, we pray out the mysteries of God. Without the Holy Spirit guiding our prayers in the Spirit, we otherwise would not know how to pray perfectly. The Holy Spirit helps us to pray a perfect prayer that coordinates completely with God's Word and also with His will for our lives. The angels gather together around as we pray out the mysteries. They are not mysteries to the angels because they hear the will of the Lord as we speak forth, and they are ready to act. Remember that when we pray in the Spirit, we actually yield to the throne room of God and His authority.

And in a similar way, the Holy Spirit takes hold of us in our human frailty to empower us in our weakness. For example, at times we don't even know how to pray, or know the best things to ask for. But the Holy Spirit rises up within us to super-intercede on our behalf, pleading to God with emotional sighs too deep for words (Romans 8:26 TPT).

When we testify by the Spirit about Jesus, we are yielding to the Spirit of prophecy (see Rev. 19:10). We are allowing the Holy Spirit to speak absolute truth from the Throne.

*But when the Helper comes, whom I shall send to you from the Father, the Spirit of truth who proceeds from the Father, He will **testify of Me**. And you also will bear witness, because you have been with Me from the beginning* (John 15:26-27).

The greatest move of the Spirit that ever will happen in the history of the world has begun. It is time for every Christian to let go of his or her life and give that life totally to God. Each Christian must make Jesus Lord over his or her entire life today. It is time to have any chains of bondage broken in every Christian's life. As every Christian yields to God, he or she releases anything that has been an anchor that keeps him or her from completely serving God. After those hindrances are gone, great things can begin to happen. Jesus had many things to say to us, but He told us that He would send the Holy Spirit to lead us into all truth. He said:

*I still have many things to say to you, but you cannot bear them now. However, when He, **the Spirit of truth, has come, He will guide you into all truth;***

for He will not speak on His own authority, but whatever He hears He will speak; and He will tell you things to come. He will glorify Me, for He will take of what is Mine and declare it to you. All things that the Father has are Mine. Therefore I said that He will take of Mine and declare it to you (John 16:12-15).

THE CHURCH

Christians have been set apart for God's purpose and therefore are sanctified by the truth (see John 17:17-19). The sooner a Christian will allow himself or herself to be caught up in the realm of the spirit in daily life, the sooner the church will rise and bring in the harvest. The angels are standing by to help implement this phase of God's eternal plan for mankind. Christians are the church of the living God, and the gates of hell shall not prevail against God's church. We are an expression of absolute truth that resides in Heaven, and we are also an expression of absolute truth that resides within each Christian on the earth through the church of the living God.

You are rising like the perfectly fitted stones of the temple; and your lives are being built up together upon the ideal foundation laid by the apostles and prophets, and best of all, you are connected to the Head Cornerstone of the building, the Anointed One, Jesus Christ himself! (Ephesians 2:20 TPT)

NOTE

1. Noah Webster's Dictionary of the English Language, 1828 edition. Public domain.

Chapter 3

The Command Center of Heaven

*Then Micaiah continued, "Listen to what the Lord says!
I saw the Lord sitting on his throne with all the armies
of heaven around him, on his right and on his left."*
—1 Kings 22:19 NLT

The Lord is indeed the God of *angel armies*. In this briefing I will explain the scene and action that is presently occurring at the *command center of Heaven*. There is a military branch of the Kingdom of God. The Lord of Hosts is in charge of all angelic activity. The strategies that are carried out on the earth are birthed at this command center. You see, angelic activity is more military than we would like to admit. The time has come for our minds to be renewed and to begin to understand those principles concerning *the agenda of angels*. The Word of God will renew and transform our minds in such a manner that we can begin to understand some of the deep things that occur in the Kingdom of Heaven. In the Book of Romans, the apostle Paul talks about the fact that we need to be transformed in our understanding.

> *And do not be conformed to this world, but be transformed by the renewing of your mind, that you may prove what is that good and acceptable and perfect will of God* (Romans 12:2).

As we submit to the Holy Spirit, the anointed Teacher who is within us, our minds begin to transform. The apostle John says:

> *But the wonderful anointing you have received from God is so much greater than their deception and now lives in you. There's no need for anyone to keep teaching you. **His anointing teaches you** all that you need to know, for it will lead you into truth, not a counterfeit. So just as the anointing has taught you, remain in him* (1 John 2:27 TPT).

Our worldview will encounter great change when we allow the mighty Holy Spirit to implement the absolute truth and help to renew our viewpoint from a human perspective to a perspective that is more divine. The absolute truth that the Holy Spirit begins to reveal to us begins at the seat of power of Heaven.

The *command center of Heaven* will receive the absolute truth of the throne room, thus enabling strategies to be set into motion to help us have victory in each particular case and challenge that we may face. This procedure is similar to the process followed today by the military. The first step is to gather intelligence. The next step is to formulate a plan of execution. Here is a scenario recorded in Scripture that reveals what types of things are happening behind the scenes to address the planning of strategies for angels.

> *And Micaiah said, Hear the word of the Lord: I saw the Lord sitting on His throne, and all the host of heaven standing by Him on His right hand and on His left. And the Lord said, Who will entice Ahab to go up and fall at Ramoth-gilead? One said this way, another said that way.* **Then there came forth a spirit [of whom I am about to tell] and stood before the Lord and said, I will entice him. The Lord said to him, By what means? And he said, I will go forth and be a lying spirit in the mouths of all his prophets. [The Lord] said, You shall entice him and succeed also. Go forth and do it.** *So the Lord has put a lying spirit in the mouths of all these prophets; and the Lord has spoken evil concerning you* (1 Kings 22:19-23 AMPC).

The Lord has planned strategies for bringing victory in every challenge that we face on this earth. The Lord has preordained times and seasons, and He continually gives information concerning them to His angels. In Acts 1:7 Jesus states, "The Father is the one who sets the fixed dates and the times of their fulfillment. You are not permitted to know the timing of all that he has prepared by his own authority" (TPT). We need to pray and ask God to reveal His plans to us. We also need to pray and ask Him to give us wisdom so that we are ready to do our part to fulfill those things that He desires. The fulfillment of His desires will occur in our present time. The time in which we now live is actually the end of this dispensation. That means that we have entered into the time when the whole earth is being filled with His glory.

PENTAGON BRIEFING

Several years ago, I had one of the most profound visitations involving angels that I have ever experienced. The visitation involved revelation of things to come that are still coming to pass at this present time. On December 6, 2014, the Lord told me to go to Washington, D.C. I stayed there one night in the Doubletree Hotel, which is across from the Pentagon. When I obeyed the Lord and made the trip to Washington, angels appeared. There were six angels in total, and when they appeared, they gave me instruction. I thought, "Who is ever going to believe that this has actually happened to me?" I was trying to picture myself telling somebody all about this angelic visitation. I said to myself, "There's just no way that I am ever going to convince anyone that what is happening now really occurred."

In my church, the things that those angels told me were going to happen did occur. In my life, the things that those angels told me did occur. Everything that those angels spoke did, in fact, occur. It was so perfect. But the one thing that the angels told me was this: "Kevin, you completely understand what we are revealing to you. That is why when we heard you were coming, we could not wait to talk to you! We know that you understand how important it is to obey and do what God asks you to do. We know that you will drop everything that you are doing to participate in what God calls you to do. You are not going to wait for a coming move of God because you understand that the move of God has already begun; it is already here. You are going to start seeing this move of God in your church." This was in December. "You are going to start seeing miracles, you are going to start seeing the manifestation of God. Be obedient."

Everything the angels told me is happening presently.

These angels said, "Listen, we were given these sacred things and sent down here to give these to you. These books are sacred; they are from a bookshelf that is located in Heaven. Your testimony is already written." The angels showed me how they bring the information to the earth. There is a veil. They just took these beautiful gold ornamented boxes that are gifts from God and passed them through the veil, instructing, "Take them." I took them into my hand. They said, "These are for you. No one else is to touch them."

Then they said, "Can you just raise your hands and worship God? We just love it when you worship God with no music. You do not even need music or anything; you just lift your hands and you start worshiping God as though you are in front of the throne." So, I did. I started worshiping. They all raised their hands and worshiped with me. I pondered, "Is this really happening?" They made the request, "Can you just worship God like you do? We just love how you can worship God without having music or anything."

I guess there is something special that happens when human beings worship God. Our worship of Him is different to God than the worship of angels. Angels worship all the time. Worship is part of what they continually do. They are always worshiping, they are always joyful, and they are always excited about what God is doing. They try to relay their fervor and passion for God and His Kingdom to Christians here on earth, but they do not achieve results quickly with everyone. They are persistent to see their purpose through because they want God's plan fulfilled for each of us. When angels find people who respond and do what is right, they congregate. A Christian can attract the activity of angels by responding to God in obedience and worshiping Him in Spirit and in truth. Angels constantly seek to find people who desire to participate in what has begun to come upon this earth in this present age.

Angels are looking for people who will actually just start participating in the move now, before it even goes to full manifestation. They are searching for people who will just start to walk in the glory of God now. Angels will seek for those who are dwelling in God's glory now, and they are capable of making it easier for us to move in the things of God. They will help a Christian to such a great degree that other people will begin to wonder how those Christians are doing what they are doing. That a Christian is capable of moving so well in the things he or she does will be a result of God showing favor upon that Christian. God shows great favor to Christians who have chosen to allow Him to come into their lives and rule as Lord. Angels can do so much to assist Christians in fulfilling the destiny that God has ordained for them. Angels are sent to Christians to help them become victorious in those things that will truly count for the Kingdom of God.

One of those angels made a very profound statement to me. The angel said that personnel at the Pentagon did not know that the angels would, that very day, be influencing the policies of this country, the United States. When I asked if they would accompany me home, the angels said that they could not come with me. They stated that they were assigned to the Pentagon and must stay at the Pentagon. They told me that God required the angels to influence the policies of the Pentagon, and that some of those polices included the nation of Israel.

Two Enemies

Next, the angels explained that the next move of God has already begun. They said that the special forces of God's military and the equipment for those forces were already present on the earth. These forces and equipment were in position for the next move of God. They told me that we were not to wait any longer for the next move of God because we were about to enter into that move at that very time. They also they told me there were two enemies against this move of God. These enemies were going to try to work against the glory of God coming forth upon the earth. The two enemies of the glory are:

1. *Lack of healing of the soul (mind, will, and emotions) of the church leadership*

The leadership of the churches must allow the Holy Spirit to heal them. There are many of God's people who have experienced traumatic events and need recovery immediately. To demonstrate this truth, the angels took me to a church that I knew. They showed me the leadership ministering to the congregation. The glory of God came into the church and was poured out into the leadership of the church. But to my dismay, I saw that those in leadership had large holes all over their bodies. Through those holes, the glory of God was pouring out of their bodies. Because these leaders were not able to carry the glory, it leaked through the holes that their bodies contained. These leaders were unable to access the glory that God had poured out to minister to the people who were standing to receive from God. These angels explained that what I was witnessing was the inability of these leaders to hold God's glory because of the lack of healing in these leaders. If these leaders were able to receive healing, then they would be fully able to hold God's glory and distribute it to those in need of that glory. God's glory poured out into the people was essential to the people because it was meant to assist them in receiving the answer to their problems.

2. *Merchandising and sensational display of the move of the glory of the Father*

The angels showed me the Ark of the Covenant from the Old Testament. It was a beautiful piece of furniture made of gold and wood. I saw the Ark upon a cart. The Ark did not have the poles with which it was supposed to be carried. The angels explained to me that when one sees the Ark of His Presence upon a cart, it has a special meaning. The Ark upon a cart without the poles symbolizes that the move of God has been merchandised and that it has been put upon display for sensationalism. When the move of the Lord has been merchandised and put on display to create sensationalism then the move of the Lord is fully aborted. The move of God is totally lost; it is rendered null and void. The people of God must learn to carry the presence of God properly. Christians must carry the move of God in the way that the Lord God had instructed them to carry it. In the Old Testament times, the Ark was carried by priests who were trained and set apart for God's purposes. These priests knew this fact: poles were essential for carrying the Ark as God instructed.

During this particular visitation of angels during that evening in Washington, D.C., I was transformed by the revelation of God. I am still, to this very day, being influenced by the instruction that those angels imparted to me. I began to clearly comprehend that the glory of God will continue to increase on the earth and that the membrane between the spirit realm and the physical realm is but a thin veil. I also saw the great possibility that God can choose His own, His children, to implement the sacred things of God. As His own, we can implement a move of God that He provides for our generation. Because of the revelation of the way God intends to use His people, I am thoroughly convinced that we, His people, are being called to a separate life with God. Christians are called to walk with their Father God in holiness.

I realize now that the enemy of our souls is continually, relentlessly trying to keep leadership relegated to a small place. The enemy attempts to contain Christian leadership to a small place through the use of traumatic events in our lives. These events are ones that are not easily resolved, nor are they easily healed. And, of course, the enemy of our souls capitalizes upon the temptation Christians can possess. That temptation is to sensationalize the move of God and to also merchandise that move of God. Why is the enemy able to capitalize on this temptation? He is capable of doing this because he realizes that he can control the move of God if he can cause Christian leaders to fail to walk in holiness. Selfishness causes these Christian leaders to succumb to the temptation to sensationalize and merchandise God's divine move. These leaders fail to recognize that all of the glory for victory belongs to the Lord God, not to the leaders themselves.

In these last days, to avoid the pitfalls of attempting to merchandise or to sensationalize God's move, Christian leaders must seek God. They must seek Him in everything they are doing, and they must seek Him in every way possible. By following after the Lord and maintaining honor, respect, and holiness toward the things of the Lord, these Christian leaders will thereby prepare themselves to enter into the greatest move of God that has ever occurred upon the earth. Christian leaders must allow the Holy Spirit to open our eyes to comprehend what God has destined for each life, as it is written in the books in Heaven that record our divine destiny. As a Christian leader begins to understand the divine destiny for himself or herself, according to Psalm 139:16, then that leader can begin to enter fully into the move that the Lord has begun. The Holy Spirit, as master of the spirit realm, will then be able reveal our future to us. The Spirit of God wants to fully inform Christian leaders concerning not only angelic secret military briefings, but also angelic activity amongst us. Angelic secret military briefings and angelic activity are both present for us to experience within the great move of the Lord in last days of this dispensation.

EYES THAT SEE

So much written concerning each Christian has not yet been fulfilled. Frequently, fulfillment is not forthcoming because it is more than our finite understanding can fully comprehend. Paul wrote to the Corinthian church to share the idea that what God desires for His children has not even entered our minds. Paul says that ear has not heard, eye has not seen what God has planned for those who love Him! Paul states that the good things of God for us are so great that we cannot possibly fully comprehend what He desires to pour out upon our lives. The verse below explains this situation for our understanding:

> *But, on the contrary, as the Scripture says, What eye has not seen and ear has not heard and has not entered into the heart of man, [all that] God has prepared (made and keeps ready) for those who love Him [who hold Him in affectionate reverence, promptly obeying Him and gratefully recognizing the benefits He has bestowed]* (1 Corinthians 2:9 AMPC).

It is time for the eyes of every Christian to be open and to recognize the things of God. Christians must begin to see into the spirit realm through faith. Our heavenly Father loves us affectionately. The Lord has laid up many benefits for His own. Through Christ Jesus, the benefits that God has prepared come to Christians. We must understand that the Lord God Almighty is in command of Heaven's army. We must be cognizant of the truth that He is about to do great wonders in our midst. It is time that Christians' eyes begin to see and that Christians' ears begin to hear the word of the Lord. Now is the time for Christians to see the great and mighty wonders of God coming to pass before their very eyes.

HEAR THE WORD OF THE LORD AS THE SPIRIT SPEAKS. THE WORD OF THE LORD TO YOU IS THAT THERE IS FREEDOM WHERE THE SPIRIT

OF THE LORD IS. THERE IS UNDERSTANDING
WHERE THE SPIRIT OF THE LORD IS. THERE
IS PERFECT LOVE THAT DRIVES OUT FEAR
WHERE THE SPIRIT OF THE LORD IS. THERE IS
ABUNDANT PROVISION WHERE THE SPIRIT OF
THE LORD IS. WORSHIP AT THE FEET OF THE
COMMANDER OF ANGEL ARMIES. FOR HE IS
WORTHY!

THE COMMANDER

The most important person in the command center of Heaven is the Lord Himself. He is in charge. He possesses full authority. All the angels harken to His voice continually. They stand and await for the next command from the Commander of Heaven.

> *Here he comes! The Commander! The mighty Lord of Angel Armies is on our side. The God of Jacob fights for us! Pause in his presence. Everyone look! Come and see the breathtaking wonders of our God. For he brings both ruin and revival. He's the one who makes conflicts end throughout the earth, breaking and burning every weapon of war. Surrender your anxiety! Be silent and stop your striving and you will see that I am God. I am the God above all the nations, and I will be exalted throughout the whole earth. Here he stands! The Commander! The mighty Lord*

of Angel Armies is on our side! The God of Jacob fights for us! Pause in his presence (Psalm 46:7-11 TPT).

At this present time, each and every Christian must relinquish his or her will to the Lord, the God of Angel armies. The revelation of the Spirit in this day and this hour is this: that Christians honor the Father, the One who sits on the throne in absolute authority. Christians must come to the knowledge that God, despite His divine authority, chooses to include every Christian as an active agent of His divine plan. His desire is that His children have a very large and distinct part in this final end-time harvest. No one in the command center of Heaven challenges the Lord. Our God is full of glory. Christians must recognize the need for our Commander to come and reveal Himself to us. The psalmist explains it this way: "Revive us, O God! Let your beaming face shine upon us with the sunrise rays of glory; then nothing will be able to stop us. O God, the mighty Commander of Angel Armies, how much longer will you smolder in anger?" (Ps. 80:3-4 TPT).

> *Can you hear it? Heaven is filled with your praises, O Lord! All the holy ones are praising you for your miracles. The sons of God are all praising you for your mighty wonders. We could search the skies forever and never find one like you. All the mighty angels could not be compared to you. You are a God who is greatly to be feared as you preside over the council of holy ones. You are surrounded by trembling ones Who are overwhelmed with fear and dread, Stunned as they stand in awe of you! So awesome are you, O Yahweh, Lord God of Angel Armies! Where could we find anyone as*

glorious as you? Your faithfulness shines all around you! (Psalm 89:5-8 TPT)

There are a number of truths revealed in the above verses of Psalms that Christians must begin to acknowledge. Christians must concentrate on the Commander of the angel armies. It is essential that Christians begin to fully grasp basic understandings of the principles of the command center of Heaven. The assignments of every Christian upon this earth are powerful. Those assignments include working with angels in this present and final move of God. Here are four very important briefings:

1. **Briefing one: Heaven is filled with Your praises, O Lord!**

    - All the holy ones are praising You for Your miracles.

    - The sons of God are all praising You for Your mighty wonders.

    - We could search the skies forever and never find one like You.

2. **Briefing two: All the mighty angels could not be compared to You.**

    - You are a God who is greatly to be feared as You preside over the council of holy ones.

    - You are surrounded by trembling ones who are overwhelmed with fear and dread, stunned as they stand in awe of You!

3. **Briefing three: So awesome are You, O Yahweh, Lord God of Angel Armies!**

- Where could we find anyone as glorious as You?

- Your faithfulness shines all around You!

Briefing one states that all of Heaven is praising the God of Angel armies. As the angels stand around Him; the holy ones are praising the Lord for the miracles that He performs. These angels confirm that He is the Almighty God, the Worker of Miracles. Not one of the angels is deceived into thinking that they have the power to do miracles without Him. He performed signs and wonders because that is His divine personality and part of His divine character.

With the Lord, miracles and wonders occur naturally. Christians must preach the Word of God. Then, and only then, will signs follow the preaching of Christians. We are His holy ones; we are His saints. The angels also are His holy ones. Angels faithfully carry out His commands. This present and final move of God will come forth with more and more strength as Christians discern the Lord in all humility. The angels discern the Lord in all humility, and Christians must discern Him in all humility also! *Strong's Concordance* defines three terms that are important when considering briefing one. Christians must begin to fully comprehend these three terms:

1. פֶּלֶא—pele, miracle (H6382)

Strong's dictionary definition: from H6381; a miracle—marvelous thing, wonder (-ful, -fully).

AV (13)—wonder 8, wonderful 3, wonderfully 1, marvelous 1; wonder, marvel.

Wonder (extraordinary, hard to understand thing) wonder (of God's acts of judgment and redemption).

2. קָדוֹשׁ—qadosh, Holy Ones (H6918)

Strong's dictionary definition: from H6942; sacred (ceremonially or morally); (as noun) God (by eminence), an angel, a saint, a sanctuary—holy (One), saint.

AV (116)—holy 65, Holy One 39, saint 12.

Sacred, holy, Holy One, saint, set apart.

3. עָרַךְ—ârak, array for battle, search to compare (H6186)

Strong's dictionary definition: a primitive root; to set in a row, i.e. arrange, put in order (in a very wide variety of applications)—put (set) (the battle, self) in array, compare, direct, equal, esteem, estimate, expert (in war), furnish, handle, join (battle), ordain, (lay, put, reckon up, set) (in) order, prepare, tax, value.

AV (75)—array 26, order 21, prepare 5, expert 3, value 3, compare 2, direct 2, equal 2, estimate 2, furnish 2, ordained 2, misc 4.

To arrange, set or put or lay in order, set in array, prepare, order, ordain, handle, furnish, esteem, equal, direct, compare (Qal) to arrange or set or lay in order, arrange, state in order, set forth (a legal case), set in place to compare, be comparable (Hiphil) to value, tax.

Can you see the angels standing around the Lord God Almighty; the holy ones are praising Him in a holy array for battle.

They praise their Commander for the miracles He performs. To the angels, *He is the Almighty God, the Worker of Miracles.*

Briefing two explains that no one in the command center, or anywhere else in the universe for that matter, can be compared to our Lord. He is our Commander. He presides over all the holy ones, and that includes both His saints and His angels. There is a council of the holy ones present with God. That council of holy ones surround Him. That council is trembling, overwhelmed with fear and dread because they know that He is so awesome and worthy to be worshiped. Imagine being completely stunned in the divine presence of the Lord God Almighty. He truly is the Commander of the His army. As Commander of His army, the Lord sets the agenda of the angels. The angels tremble in awe of the power of the Lord. Christians must begin to comprehend that what our angels are experiencing at the throne at this very time is far beyond our finite understanding. In order to work with Heaven and God's holy messengers, Christians must begin to recognize that God is awesome and worthy to be worshiped, and that His presence causes even the angels around Him to tremble because our God is the awesome and powerful Almighty God, to whom nothing is impossible.

Strong's Concordance defines two terms that are important when considering briefing two. Christians must begin to fully comprehend these two terms:

1. עָרַץ—âraş, greatly feared (H6206)

Strong's dictionary definition: a primitive root; to awe or (intransitive) to dread; hence, to harass—be affrighted (afraid, dread, feared, terrified), break, dread, fear, oppress, prevail, to shake terribly.

AV (15)—afraid 3, fear 3, dread 2, terribly 2, break 1, affrighted 1, oppress 1, prevail 1, terrified 1.

To tremble, dread, fear, oppress, prevail, break, be terrified, cause to tremble (Qal) to cause to tremble, terrify to tremble, feel dread (Niphal) to be awesome, be terrible (Hiphil) to regard or treat with awe, regard or treat as awful to inspire with awe, terrify.

2. אֵרֵא—yârê, reverence of the trembling ones (H3372)

Strong's dictionary definition: a primitive root; to fear; morally, to revere; caus. to frighten—affright, be (make) afraid, dread (-ful), (put in) fear (-ful, -fully, -ing), (be had in) reverence (-end), x see, terrible (act, -ness, thing).

AV (314)—fear 188, afraid 78, terrible 23, terrible thing 6, dreadful 5, reverence 3, fearful 2, terrible acts 1, misc 8

To fear, revere, be afraid (Qal) to fear, be afraid to stand in awe of, be awe, to fear, reverence, honor, respect (Niphal) to be fearful, be dreadful, be feared to cause astonishment and awe, be held in awe to inspire reverence or godly fear.

You can understand that we need to comprehend in our own lives, these characteristics of the angel's response to a holy God. The tremble and have an awesome reverence and fear for the presence and glory of God.

In *briefing three*, we understand that in God's awesome presence, we are able to see His glory revealed. The very Person of God the Father is His glory. Part of that glory is Jesus Christ. Jesus is the exact representation of the Father. The angels are so bright because they are energized and receive strength from Him. They willingly and joyfully do their Commander's will. Angels are faithful to Him who sits on the throne of all authority. This is why the psalmist refers to God's faithfulness surrounding Him. His angels are the "faithful ones." Christians are part of this implementation of God's faithfulness as well. Christians do His will with the help of the Holy Spirit and His angels.

Strong's Concordance defines three terms that are important when considering briefing three. Christians must begin to fully comprehend these three terms:

1. חָסִין—ḥăsîyn, awesome (H2626)

Strong's dictionary definition: from 2630; properly, firm, i.e. (by implication) mighty—strong.

AV (1)—strong 1.

Strong, mighty.

2. כָּבוֹד—ḵâḇôḏ, glorious (H3519)

Strong's dictionary definition: from H3513; properly, weight, but only figuratively in a good sense, splendor or copiousness—glorious (-ly), glory, honor (-able).

AV (200)—glory 156, honor 32, glorious 10, gloriously 1, honorable 1.

Glory, honor, glorious, abundance, riches honor, splendor, glory honor, dignity honor, reputation honor, reverence, glory.

3. אֱמוּנָה—emûnâ, faithfulness (H530)

Strong's dictionary definition: feminine of 529; literally firmness; figuratively security; morally fidelity—faith (-ful, -ly, -ness, (man)), set office, stability, steady, truly, truth, verily.

AV (49)—faithfulness 18, truth 13, faithfully 5, office 5, faithful 3, faith 1, stability 1, steady 1, truly 1, verily 1. Firmness, fidelity, steadfastness, steadiness.

We need to meditate on the awesomeness of God's glory that surrounds Him. The time we spend waiting before Him will allow us to comprehend His faithfulness to us. Angels certainly are aware of His glory and are agents of His faithfulness toward us. Never doubt that God is faithful. He loves His people and will not forget His covenant with them. *He is the Lord of Heaven's Armies!*

> *Then David again gathered all the elite troops in Israel, 30,000 in all. He led them to Baalah of Judah to bring back the Ark of God, which bears the name of the Lord of Heaven's Armies, who is enthroned between the cherubim* (2 Samuel 6:1-2 NLT).

Chapter 4

THE FEAR OF THE LORD

Therefore, having these promises, beloved, let us cleanse ourselves from all filthiness of the flesh and spirit, perfecting holiness in the fear of God.
—2 CORINTHIANS 7:1

At this present time and dispensation, one of the most important aspects to consider when discussing angels and angel visitation is this crucial subject—the *fear of the Lord*. When angels visit, they bring the presence of God with them, and one can definitely sense the fear of God. Few of the people who are asking the Lord for an encounter with angels have any understanding of the awesome power of God that such an encounter will include. Those who seek such encounters do not anticipate the fact that meeting with angels will definitely bring one to a brand-new level of comprehension of what the fear of the Lord actually means. Such a visitation of angels will yield far more understanding of God's awesome power than anyone could imagine. When a person receives a response to his or her query to have an angelic visitation, he or she will definitely have a totally new level of respect for the unexpected things of God. He or she will have a transformed view of the power of God. Once a person has been in the presence of His angels, he or she will have a new, more comprehensive view and understanding of the fear of the Lord.

When I experience the presence of angels, I receive a totally new level of understanding of the *fear of the Lord*. One may wonder why angels bring such a presence of God with them when they visit mankind. It is important to recognize that these very angels have just left the presence of the Lord in the throne room of Heaven. They have just been in the presence of God Almighty. They come from a realm outside of most of our experiences, the realm called the Kingdom of Heaven. This Kingdom is full of authority and power. Our flesh cannot always handle the degree of authority and power that one encounters when angels appear.

The importance and influence of the holiness of the Lord is not always something foremost in a Christian's mind. Born-again believers often forget that angels are holy beings. That is why they are called *holy* angels. We are in a fallen world, and although our spirit is born anew, our bodies have not yet been redeemed.

Angels' bodies can handle the power and presence of God because the Lord created them with the capacity to stand in His power and presence. But Christians' human bodies can only handle a certain degree of that power and presence of the Lord Almighty. Not only our bodies but also our minds need transformation and renewing by the Word of God (see Rom. 12:2). Angels' minds are created with a capacity to fully receive the *absolute truth* that flows from Heaven. Angels, unlike mankind, do not encounter resistance to God's truth because they are not, as mankind, fallen beings.

The encounters with angels that I have personally experienced also revealed to me the fact that human beings often are not prepared for the visitation of angels into one's life! For example, I was so interested in encountering one of these beings; however, in my desire to experience the presence of angels, I failed to recognize what I would experience when the angels did come to visit me. I did not realize that I would not have a great capacity to handle that visitation. In fact, when that first angel appeared in my room, I fell down as dead. I was unable to move until he came over and helped me up! The holiness and the fear of the Lord that was on that angel was much greater than my capacity to a stand in his presence.

I have discovered that the human body lacks the ability to withstand the power and presence that is upon angels when they appear. Nevertheless, there is a key to being prepared for the visitation of angels. The key is the *fear of the Lord*. The fear of the Lord begins when a person comprehends a new level of God's holiness. As one begins to encounter the truth of holiness and the true fear of the Lord, he or she is then better able to handle more of what the Lord has prepared for him or her in that personal and unique relationship with Him. The relationship that God has prepared for every Christian includes the following three essential elements:

- Revelation
- Visitation
- Habitation

These three elements must come in a specific order. The Lord will use these elements to edify His saints and help them to possess the ability to walk with God as Enoch walked with God. Enoch walked with God *before he was taken*. Enoch is a type of the church. Enoch pleased God, and then he was taken up into the heavens. God gave us this revelation to show us that when the church of Christ pleases the Lord, the church will then also be prepared, as Enoch was prepared, to be taken up into the heavens.

> *Faith lifted Enoch from this life and he was taken up into heaven! He never had to experience death; he just disappeared from this world because God promoted him. For before he was translated to the heavenly realm his life had become a pleasure to God. And without faith living within us it would be impossible to please God. For we come to God in faith knowing that he is real and that he rewards the faith of those who give all their passion and strength into seeking him* (Hebrews 11:5-6 TPT).

When a Christian initiates the first element of this process, which is the stage of *revelation*, into his or her relationship with God on a continual basis, he or she will then be prepared to enter into the second element of the process, *visitation*. Next, he or she will enter into the third phase of the process, which is *habitation*. The third process of habitation will come swiftly after visitation. Once a Christian has gone through the three elements of revelation, visitation, and habitation, then a solid foundation has been established, and he or she will be able to permanently abide in these places of authority and experience. Once a person is firmly established in authority and experience, he or she will also walk with confidence, established in the fear of the Lord. This is part of the agenda that God has assigned to angels—the implementation of a greater understanding of the fear of the Lord in the Christian's life.

PHASE ONE: REVELATION

Revelation is the first phase of this process. Revelation involves both the ministry of the Holy Spirit and the Word of God. As the ministry of the Holy Spirit and the Word of God band together in a person's spirit, that person's mind begins to yield to the Holy Spirit. As a result of yielding to the Holy Spirit, transformation begins to happen within a person's mind, and that person's understanding becomes enlightened by the Holy Spirit and the Word. The Holy Spirit's objective is to reveal Jesus to each person. The Holy Spirit desires to attain revelation of Christ in every Christian's life. The Holy Spirit takes what the Father has freely given to Him and then gives it to the yielded Christian. The Holy Spirit will remind a Christian of the things that Jesus has said, and He will even at times reveal the future to Christians who are yielded to the Lord.

In the phase of revelation, a Christian will start to see the mysteries of God as the Holy Spirit uncovers them. That is why it is very important for a Christian to be totally focused upon the absolute truth. The truth is within God's Word. In meditating upon this absolute truth found in the Word, a Christian begins to pray in the Holy Spirit. The Holy Spirit's edification, or building up, of a Christian's spirit will cause the development of maturity in faith. This faith is renewed and strengthened trust in God as a Person. As this process continues, a Christian develops his or her relationship with the Lord to such an extent that the person begins to have absolute confidence that the Lord is a God who always does what He says He will do. According to Jude 20, this type of edification of a person's relationship with the Lord works to build up a renewed faith. The type of faith that comes forth then becomes holy and sanctified to such a degree that that faith cannot be destroyed.

In my own life, I have undergone this process. As a Christian prays in the spirit and meditates upon the Word of God, his or her life is beginning to set them apart from those Christians who have not undergone this process. The actual "setting apart" begins to renew a person's spirit and then proceeds to renew a person's mind. A Christian who has begun this process starts to walk in the fear of the Lord. That particular Christian becomes keenly aware, as never before that time, and he or she begins to realize that God truly is an all-knowing and an all-seeing Father. A Christian's fear of the Lord increases as this revelation phase opens more and more understanding to him or her. As a Christian progresses further and further into this process of revelation, he or she begins to understand the character of the Lord more and more. The fear of the Lord is the beginning of this understanding. "The fear of the Lord is the beginning of wisdom; a good understanding have all those who do His commandments. His praise endures forever" (Ps. 111:10).

It is of vital importance that Christians begin to understand that the fear of the Lord is essential to our lives. The fear of the Lord is necessary because without that revelation a Christian is unlikely to be an active participant in the move of God that has already begun on the earth today. This revelation phase will start to take place just as it did in the early church, and it will continually occur until the Lord Jesus returns to meet us in the air. Solomon wrote that people must have the fear of the Lord. Solomon knew that God's people must have revelation concerning the holiness of our God in order to have wisdom. Solomon also knew that it was essential that God's chosen people have an understanding of the importance of the fear of the Lord. "The fear of the Lord is the beginning of wisdom, and the knowledge of the Holy One is understanding" (Prov. 9:10).

Jesus has stated that the Spirit will lead a Christian into all truth. The revelation of the Spirit must take us into the deeper things of God. One of the important things that we must understand as Christians is the *fear of the Lord*. God's character is far above that which Christians have discerned. Some Christians believe that they have comprehended so much of the Lord, but they would probably be extremely surprised to find out that they are merely in the first phase of the process. They will be shocked to realize that the Holy Spirit will lead them to a much deeper understanding. That deeper understanding will be their initial understanding of the fullness of the *fear of the Lord* in holiness and what it actually represents.

Christians have been bought with the great price of Christ's atonement. When a Christian truly submits to the lordship of Christ, he or she belongs to the Lord. A Christian may fail to recognize that God has redeemed him or her and that the Lord truly counts him or her as His possession. No other part of all of God's creation has been redeemed by the Lord. Only human beings have been purchased with His blood. If any Christian wants to move forward and move through this first phase called revelation, then he or she must learn the true definition of holiness and the true definition of fear of the Lord. God is jealous over His own. It is His desire to have a Christian for Himself. He wants every one of His own to become separated from the world. Revelation brings a Christian into a new understanding of the fear of the Lord, and that fear of the Lord is the beginning of wisdom.

The early church demonstrated Christians in this first phase of revelation. Right after the Holy Spirit was poured out upon His saints, Christians began to move in the revelation of who they were in Christ. In a very short period of time, multitudes came into the Kingdom of God. These Christians received the Word of God and were baptized. The Holy Spirit came upon them. This combination caused revelation as well as manifestation.

> *And with many other words he testified and exhorted them, saying, "Be saved from this perverse genera-tion." Then those who gladly received his word were baptized; and that day about three thousand souls were added to them. And they continued steadfastly in the apostles' doctrine and fellowship, in the break-ing of bread, and in prayers. **Then fear came upon every soul, and many wonders and signs were done through the apostles** (Acts 2:40-43).*

PHASE TWO: VISITATION

The next phase of the move of God is *visitation*. During the phase of visitation, people begin to think of others rather than them-selves. The fear of the Lord inspires such action. It is not surprising that angels also begin to minister in supernatural ways. Provision that is supernatural will happen. Unity and selflessness will begin to rule the church. The Book of Acts states that, "All the believers were one in mind and heart. Selfishness was not a part of their community, for they shared everything they had with one another" (Acts 4:32 TPT).

So the individual believer will encounter visitation, and that visitation will continue to change each of them. The real test of this phase is that visitation begins to influence the lives of others. Then there is a division among believers that will begin. There will be those people who will not continue to go forward with the visitation in a corporate setting. As a result, the Holy Spirit will visit us individually in a wonderful way. As revelation and visitation of the Lord increases, the corporate meeting becomes more and more powerful. The source of that power is the unity amongst believers.

When some believers fail to understand the *fear of the Lord*, a division begins. The Lord wants each Christian to judge himself or herself so that each is not judged by God. The following passage of Scripture demonstrates this point very well. Visitation can cause judgment to occur, especially if any Christian does not learn of the holiness of the Lord and fails to permit the Holy Spirit to set him or her apart as a holy people.

> *Now, a man named Ananias and his wife, Sapphira, likewise sold their farm. They conspired to secretly keep back for themselves a portion of the proceeds. So when Ananias brought the money to the apostles, it was only a portion of the entire sale. God revealed their secret to Peter, so he said to him, "Ananias, why did you let Satan fill your heart and make you think you could lie to the Holy Spirit? You only pretended to give it all, yet you hid back part of the proceeds from the sale of your property to keep for yourselves. Before you sold it,*

wasn't it yours to sell or to keep? And after you sold it, wasn't the money entirely at your disposal? How could you plot such a thing in your heart? You haven't lied to people; you've lied to God!"

The moment Ananias heard those words, he fell over dead. Everyone was terrified when they heard what had happened. Some young men came in and removed the body and buried him.

Three hours later, his wife came into the room, with no clue what had happened to her husband. Peter said to her, "Tell me, were the two of you paid this amount for the sale of your land?" Sapphira said, "Yes, that's how much it was." Peter told her, "Why have you agreed together to test the Spirit of the Lord? I hear the footsteps of those who buried your husband at the door—they're coming here to bury you too!" At that moment she dropped dead at Peter's feet. When the young men came in, she was already dead, so they carried her out and buried her next to her husband. **The entire church was seized with a powerful sense of the fear of God, which came over all who heard what had happened.**

The apostles performed many signs, wonders, and miracles among the people. And the believers were wonderfully united as they met regularly in the temple courts in the area known as Solomon's Porch. No one dared harm them, for everyone held them in high regard.

Continually more and more people believed in the Lord and were added to their number—great crowds of both men and women. In fact, when people knew Peter was going to walk by, they carried the sick out to the streets and laid them down on cots and mats, knowing the incredible power emanating from him would overshadow them and heal them. Great numbers of people swarmed into Jerusalem from the nearby villages. They brought with them the sick and those troubled by demons—and everyone was healed! (Acts 5:1-16 TPT)

Yet there were many in the crowd who believed the message, bringing the total number of men who believed to nearly five thousand! (Acts 4:4 TPT)

The fear of the Lord fell on them and many signs and wonders and miracles were performed. However, two church members died early, and they did not need to die at such an early age. The *agenda of angels* is to bring us into an understanding of the holiness of God and the fear of the Lord. Christians are to move into deeper understanding of the Lord and His holiness. The *agenda of angels* also involves miracles; signs and wonders will appear. Presently, the fear of the Lord is returning as revelation to the church.

When Christians pray for a move of God to happen, Christians must realize that the move must start with us individually as we enter into the revelation phase of the Spirit of God. As we judge ourselves and mature, we influence others to judge themselves. Our actions that are a response to our renewed understanding of the holiness of God can begin a domino effect in the spirit as well as in this physical realm. Visitation will then bring an even greater degree of the *fear of the Lord* into each Christian's life. Visitation then begins to move to a much higher level. The anointing of God will increase to an extreme level amongst any group of people who encounter a unity of visitation with revelation.

When that anointing increases due to the unity resulting from visitation and revelation, people will desire to gather together with those who have that unity. Answers to prayer will occur, and mighty miracles will be brought forth. In this second stage, Christians will realize both the importance of seeking communion with believers and the importance of coming out and being separate from unbelievers. The apostle Paul said:

> *Do not be unequally yoked together with unbelievers. For what fellowship has righteousness with lawlessness? And what communion has light with darkness? And what accord has Christ with Belial? Or what part has a believer with an unbeliever? And what agreement has the temple of God with idols? For you are the temple of the living God. As God has said: "I will dwell in them, and walk among them. I will be their God, and they shall be My people." Therefore "Come out from among them and be separate, says the Lord. Do not touch what is unclean, and I will receive you. I will be a Father to you, and you shall be My sons and daughters, says the Lord Almighty." Therefore, having these promises, beloved, let us cleanse ourselves from all filthiness of the flesh and spirit, perfecting holiness in the fear of God (2 Corinthians 6:14-7:1).*

This is a very clear picture of how we must act as Christians. This unity and fellowship must be our ultimate goal. The agreement that we can have with each other in a corporate setting will naturally cause an understanding of the fear of the Lord and the agenda of angels. The Lord desires that His children come to these important understandings; it is one of His ultimate goals for His children.

PHASE THREE: HABITATION

The ultimate goal of the angels is habitation, which is phase three of this process. They desire to be with every believer, both separately and corporately. Angels have common ground with every believer when this phase of habitation begins. The phase of habitation becomes possible only when God's people have set themselves apart and allow the fear of the Lord to complete the work of holiness in their lives. The blood of Jesus made this third process of habitation possible. This phase of habitation is truly possible but takes a great deal of time to attain. Holiness and *fear of the Lord* are essential to produce this stage of habitation.

During this final stage of habitation, unbelievers will see that the Lord is with these Christians. The favor of the Lord will over-shadow the believers, and the Holy Spirit will work mightily with God's people. The unsaved will see uncommon miracles and super-natural provision. They will give their lives to the Lord Jesus Christ in great numbers, in just the way that unbelievers gave their lives to Christ as events unfolded in the early church. They will become believers because the fear of the Lord will be revealed. During the phase called habitation, every need will be met. The Lord's ministry will be working through believers. Ministry will occur just as the Great Commission of our Lord in Mark 16 explains it is to happen.

The angels are ready to implement God's plans in the earth. They have their orders and are full of joy as they begin to visit man-kind on their missions. We are in exciting days right now. We will to see the greatest move of God that has ever occurred upon the earth, and the glory of the Lord will fully cover the earth. This is what is to happen before the coming of Jesus Christ.

There are important verses in Psalm 19 that Christians must understand. The main concentration and explanation will center upon the fear of the Lord. It is necessary to enter into this mindset concerning the fear of the Lord. Every Christian's assignment on this earth is powerful. Every Christian's assignment on this earth also includes working with angels.

There are six very important briefings that Christians need to understand found in Psalm 19; they are the following:

1. Briefing one: "The law of the Lord is perfect, converting the soul."

2. Briefing two: "The testimony of the Lord is sure, making wise the simple."

3. Briefing three: "The statutes of the Lord are right, rejoicing the heart."

4. Briefing four: "The commandment of the Lord is pure, enlightening the eyes."

5. Briefing five: "The fear of the Lord is clean, enduring forever."

6. Briefing six: "The judgments of the Lord are true and righteous altogether" (Ps. 19:7-9).

Briefing One: The law of the Lord is perfect, converting the soul.

Many of you have desired to be used of God. However, when the fear of the Lord enters your life in a stronger way by revelation, one of the first things that happens to you is that you realize that you really do not have an opinion. A previous chapter concerning absolute truth spoke of the fact that our opinion is unworthy of consideration when compared to the absolute truth of God. The fear of the Lord will bring about a higher perspective of who God is and how He does things. We want to know God by His ways, not just see His acts (see Ps. 103:7). If a Christian has the passion to know God's ways, then he or she must submit to the authority of the Lord. A believer must allow the Holy Spirit to bring the atmosphere of revelation into your life.

The Holy Spirit brings an atmosphere into a believer's presence that helps him or her to see things from God's perspective. His perspective is higher than mankind's perspective. The Holy Spirit helps Christians know the ways of God. His ways are perfect. As revelation flows from the Spirit of God, visitation begins. The overflowing power of authentic visitation not only will help a Christian to more deeply understand the Father, God Almighty. This visitation will also begin a fire of holy passion inside each Christian. The Christian will then have a strong desire to seek the Lord and draw nigh unto Him. Christians desire that God really will help them to have Him reign as Lord over their lives and that, in a sense, He will "own" them. In actuality, Christians are already under the Lord's ownership. However, there is a need for Christians to relinquish their will to Him. At the time that Christians do relinquish their will to the God of Heaven and earth, they can truly call Him Lord. King David said:

Lord, even when your path takes me through the valley of deepest darkness, fear will never conquer me, for you already have! You remain close to me and lead me through it all the way. Your authority is my strength and my peace. The comfort of your love takes away my fear. I'll never be lonely, for you are near (Psalm 23:4 TPT).

As a Christian's faith increases to more fully receive what God says as truth, then angels will gather around that person. The Word of God is living and active (see Heb. 4:12). As a Christian receives God's truth more completely, he or she will begin to move forward and follow the Lord more closely than ever before that time. And, correspondingly, as the Christian moves forward more completely into the will of God, His divine destiny for that Christian's life begins to become more completely fulfilled. "But we are not of them that shrink back unto perdition; but of them that have faith unto the saving of the soul (Heb. 10:39 ASV).

A Christian must allow God to have his or her soul as well as his or her spirit. A Christian must allow God to transform his or her soul. The soul includes the mind, the will, and the emotions. The truth that is found in the Word of God will cause the transformation of the soul. As the soul becomes transformed, that is to say that as Christians permit the *converting of the soul*, Christians are prepared to work with the agenda of angels by the Holy Spirit. The fear of the Lord will permeate a believer's soul as he or she allows God's perfect Word to have its way in his or her heart. It is important that a Christian will allow this work to begin as soon as possible in his or her life.

Briefing Two: *The testimony of the Lord is sure, making wise the simple.*

Every believer should allow the reality of the atmosphere of Heaven to permeate his or her life. One must yield to the Holy Spirit for the atmosphere of Heaven to saturate a person's life. Everything that the Lord says is absolutely steadfast. Jesus said, "The Holy Spirit is the one who gives life, that which is of the natural realm is of no help. The words I speak to you are Spirit and life. But there are still some of you who won't believe" (John 6:63 TPT). Jesus told us the Holy Spirit would come and lead us into all truth. The Spirit is speaking truth from Heaven over your life right now.

> *But when He, the Spirit of Truth (the Truth-giving Spirit) comes, He will guide you into all the Truth (the whole, full Truth). For He will not speak His own message [on His own authority]; but He will tell whatever He hears [from the Father; He will give the message that has been given to Him], and He will announce and declare to you the things that are to come [that will happen in the future]* (John 16:13 AMPC).

At this very moment, the Lord's will is clear: He desires to testify over your life. As He speaks to each Christian, He sets every one free. John 8:36 says, "So if the Son sets you free, you will be free indeed" (ESV). Paul prayed that we would have *the spirit of wisdom and revelation.* This is a vital part of participating in the move of God and assisting in the angels' missions. God is causing His chosen people to have the spirit of wisdom and revelation. He is causing this to occur on the earth right now. He, through this powerful move of His Spirit, is opening the understanding of His people to walk in revelation and in divine wisdom. Paul prayed a prayer that Christians must also pray. This prayer will help each Christian to move into his or her place in the very center of God's will for his or her life. This prayer will also help each Christian to maintain his or her place in the very center of God's will. It is important that believers pray this prayer often! Paul prayed this prayer, and Christians must also pray in the following way:

I pray that the Father of glory, the God of our Lord Jesus Christ, would impart to you [me] the riches of the Spirit of wisdom and the Spirit of revelation to know him through your [my] deepening intimacy with him.

I pray that the light of God will illuminate the eyes of your [my] imagination, flooding you [me] with light, until you [I] experience the full revelation of the hope of his calling—that is, the wealth of God's glorious inheritances that he finds in us [me], his holy ones [one]!

I pray that you [I] will continually experience the immeasurable greatness of God's power made available to you [me] through faith. Then your lives [my life] will be an advertisement of this immense power as it works through you [me]! This is the mighty power that was released when God raised Christ from the dead and exalted him to the place of highest honor and supreme authority in the heavenly realm! And now he is exalted as first above every ruler, authority, government, and realm of power in existence! He is gloriously enthroned over every name that is ever praised, not only in this age, but in the age that is coming!

And he alone is the leader and source of everything needed in the church. God has put everything beneath the authority of Jesus Christ and has given him the highest rank above all others. And now we [I], [part of] his church, are his body on the earth and that which fills him [us] who is being filled by it! (Ephesians 1:17-23 TPT)

Christians must realize that it is important to remember:

The fear of the Lord is the beginning of wisdom, and the knowledge of the Holy One is understanding (Proverbs 9:10).

Briefing Three: The statutes of the Lord are right, rejoicing the heart.

I have to announce to you that the joy of the Lord is coming with this move of the Spirit. There will be an amazing amount of oil and new wine poured out. The joy of the Lord is here. What God has established is right, and your enemy is wrong! You need to start to laugh at your impossibilities. The angels of the Lord are here to bring you into your destiny. Let every part of your life be given over to the loving heavenly Father. You will experience overflowing joy!

Trust in the Lord completely, and do not rely on your own opinions. With all your heart rely on him to guide you, and he will lead you in every decision you make. Become intimate with him in whatever you do, and he will lead you wherever you go. Don't think for a moment that you know it all, for wisdom comes when you adore him with undivided devotion and avoid everything that's wrong. Then you will find the healing refreshment your body and spirit long for. Glorify God with all your wealth, honoring him with your very best, with every increase that comes to you. **Then every dimension of your life will overflow with blessings from an uncontainable source of inner joy!** (Proverbs 3:5-10 TPT)

Briefing Four: The commandment of the Lord is pure, enlightening the eyes.

We all love the words that come from the mouth of God. They are pure and full of life, light, and truth. There is no difference between who our God is as a person and what He says from His lips. The Lord is pure, and what He says is pure. Jesus said, "Blessed are the pure in heart, for they *shall see God"* (Matt. 5:8). The Word of the Lord is pure light that enlightens the eyes of every believer to see what is before each one. Christians will see God and the spirit realm when they keep themselves pure in the fear of the Lord.

In the fear of the Lord there is strong confidence, and His children will have a place of refuge. The fear of the Lord is a fountain of life, to turn one away from the snares of death (Proverbs 14:26-27).

Briefing Five: The fear of the Lord is clean, enduring forever.

This briefing is for those who want to walk closely with the Lord in this life. The Lord will lead each Christian to walk upon holy ground. Holy ground is where the angels tread. The children of God have been called to walk with angels in this place. When the fear of the Lord is present, there is an amazing amount of fulfillment in each believer's life because He is truly all that any believer may need.

> *The fear of the Lord leads to life, and he who has it will abide in satisfaction; he will not be visited with evil* (Proverbs 19:23).

The *fear of the Lord* has many benefits. Those benefits begin when Christians bow down in humility in the presence of an awesome, holy God who loves each of His children. "By humility and the fear of the Lord are *riches and honor and life*" (Prov. 22:4). Every single Christian on earth is supposed to possess riches. That wealth has a purpose. It is provided for believers to that they are able to help the work of God. Especially in these last days, wealth is necessary for believers. The purpose of wealth is to provide a way for each Christian to continue moving forward in the things of God, ministering to others. Honor and life are part of every believer's inheritance. As Christians maintain the fear of the Lord, they will walk with angels in this last move of God. And, as Christians maintain the fear of the Lord, honor and abundant life will continue for every Christian.

> *The fear of the Lord prolongs days, but the years of the wicked will be shortened* (Proverbs 10:27).

Briefing Six: The judgments of the Lord are true and righteous altogether.

Another part of the fear of Lord is that His judgments are always right and true. If Christians are to be part of this next move of God, they must understand what God hates. Proverbs says, "The fear of the Lord is to hate evil; pride and arrogance and the evil way" (Prov. 8:13-14). We must always be cognizant of the fact that the Commander of the Lord's army, our righteous God, hates evil, pride, arrogance, and the evil way. Christians must remember that angels also hate the same things that God hates. Children of God must hate these very things as well if they desire to participate in the agenda of angels. Angels are our fellow servants, and they have been sent in these last days to serve every believer and to help every believer with the harvest of souls.

> *Therefore, having these promises, beloved, let us* **cleanse** *ourselves from all filthiness of the flesh and spirit, perfecting* **holiness** *in the* **fear** *of God* (2 Corinthians 7:1).

Second Corinthians 7:1 highlights the message of this chapter. It is an important reminder of what Paul said to the Corinthians. The following word study will emphasize the importance that all Christians must walk in holiness and also walk in the fear of the Lord.

1. καθαρίζω—katharizō, cleanse (G2511)

Strong's dictionary definition: from G2513; to cleanse (literally or figuratively)—(make) clean (-se), purge, purify.

AV (30)—cleanse 16, make clean 5, be clean 3, purge 3, purify 3.

1. to make clean

2. cleanse from physical stains and dirt

3. utensils, food

4. a leper

5. to cleanse by curing

6. to remove by cleansing

In a moral sense to free from defilement of sin and from faults to purify from wickedness to free from guilt of sin, to purify to consecrate by cleansing or purifying to consecrate, dedicate.

To pronounce clean in a Levitical sense.

2. ἁγιωσύνη—*hagiōsynē, holiness (G42)*

Strong's dictionary definition: from G40; sacredness (i.e. properly, the quality)—holiness.

AV (3)—holiness 3.

1. Majesty, holiness

2. Moral purity

3. φόβος—*phobos, fear (G5401)*

Strong's dictionary definition: from a primary φέβομαι phebomai (to be put in fear); alarm or fright—be afraid, + exceedingly, fear, terror.

AV (47)—fear 41, terror 3, misc 3.

1. Fear or dread, terror; that which strikes terror

2. Reverence for one's husband

Chapter 5

THE BEAUTY OF HOLINESS

*Ascribe to the Lord the glory due His name. Bring
an offering and come before Him; worship the Lord
in the beauty of holiness and in holy array.*
—1 CHRONICLES 16:29 AMPC

One of the most unbelievable experiences was standing before the throne room of God. Everything there was so beautiful and holy. I remember seeing Jesus Christ on His throne, beside the Father. I was not allowed to look at the face of the Father, but I experienced much glory and majesty there. I can only imagine the appearance of the Father's face. Jesus was perfect in His appearance. Everything in the throne room is beyond our human imagination. There is also great order in the holy sanctuary where the Lord dwells. The realization that all nations and peoples will have to appear before Him and give an account for the life they have lived is an astounding thought to me. Every nation and every people will know that not only is there but one true God, but also that God is holy.

I heard the saints and the angels singing and worshiping the One who sits on the throne. I saw angels beyond number, reaching as far as the eye could see. They worshiped God in white robes, and they were singing in one voice. They sang, "Worthy is the Lamb that was slain." The beauty of it all was beyond what anyone could ask or think. The Father and the Son received the worship of all people present.

> *Declare His **glory** among the nations, His marvelous works among all peoples. For great is the Lord and greatly to be praised; He also is to be [reverently] feared above all so-called gods. For all the gods of the people are [lifeless] idols, but the Lord made the heavens. **Honor** and **majesty** are [found] in His presence; strength and joy are [found] in His sanctuary. Ascribe to the Lord, you families of the peoples, ascribe to the Lord glory and strength, ascribe to the Lord the glory due His name. Bring an offering and come before Him; worship the Lord in the **beauty** of **holiness** and in holy array. **Tremble** and reverently **fear** before Him, all the earth's peoples; the*

world also shall be established, so it cannot be moved (1 Chronicles 16:24-30 AMPC).

Strong's Concordance defines five terms that are important when considering this briefing. Christians must begin to fully comprehend these five terms:

1. כָּבוֹד—*kâbôd, glory (H3519)*

Strong's dictionary definition: from H3513; properly, weight, but only figuratively in a good sense, splendor or copiousness—glorious (-ly), glory, honor (-able).

AV (200)—glory 156, honor 32, glorious 10, gloriously 1, honorable 1.

Glory, honor, glorious, abundance, riches honor, splendor, glory honor, dignity honor, reputation honor, reverence, glory.

2. הֲדָרָה—*hăḏârâ, beauty (H1927)*

Strong's dictionary definition: feminine of H1926; decoration—beauty, honor.

AV (5)—beauty 4, honor 1; adornment, glory; holy adornment (of public worship), glory (of the king).

3. קֹדֶשׁ—*qôḏeš, holiness (H6944)*

Strong's dictionary definition: from H6942; a sacred place or thing; rarely abstract, sanctity—consecrated (thing), dedicated (thing), hallowed (thing), holiness, (x most) holy (x day, portion, thing), saint, sanctuary.

AV (468)—holy 262, sanctuary 68, (holy, hallowed) things 52, most 44, holiness 30, dedicated 5, hallowed 3, consecrated 1, misc 3.

Set apart, holiness, sacredness, separateness apartness, sacredness, holiness of God of places of things.

Set apart, separateness.

4. יָרֵא—yârê, awesome splendor (H3372)

Strong's dictionary definition: a primitive root; to fear; morally, to revere; caus. to frighten—affright, be (make) afraid, dread (-ful), (put in) fear (-ful, -fully, -ing), (be had in) Reverence (-end), x see, terrible (act, -ness, thing).

AV (314)—fear 188, afraid 78, terrible 23, terrible thing 6, dreadful 5, reverence 3, fearful 2, terrible acts 1, misc 8

To fear, revere, be afraid (Qal) to fear, be afraid to stand in awe of, be awed to fear, reverence, honor, respect (Niphal) to be fearful, be dreadful, be feared to cause astonishment and awe, be held in awe to inspire reverence or godly fear.

Out of the north comes golden splendor [and people can hardly look on it]; around God is awesome splendor and majesty [far too glorious for man's eyes] (Job 37:22 AMP).

5. הוֹד—hôḏ, majesty (H1935)

Strong's dictionary definition: from an unused root; grandeur (i.e. an imposing form and appearance)—beauty, comeliness, excellence, glorious, glory, goodly, honor, majesty.

AV (24)—glory 9, honor 6, majesty 4, beauty 1, comeliness 1, glorious 1, goodly 1, honorable 1.

Splendor, majesty, vigor.

Proclaim his majesty, all you mighty champions, you sons of Almighty God, giving all the glory and strength back to him! Be in awe before his majesty. Be in awe before such power and might! Come worship wonderful Yahweh, arrayed in all his splendor, bowing in worship as he appears in all his holy beauty. Give him the honor due his name. Worship him wearing the glory-garments of your holy, priestly calling! The voice of the Lord echoes through the skies and seas. The Glory-God reigns as he thunders in the clouds. So powerful is his voice, so brilliant and bright, how majestic as he thunders over the great waters! His tympanic thunder topples the strongest of trees. His symphonic sound splinters the mighty forests. Now he moves Zion's mountains by the might of his voice, shaking the snowy peaks with his ear-splitting sound! The lightning-fire flashes, striking as he speaks. God reveals himself when he makes the fault lines quake, shaking deserts, speaking his voice. God's mighty voice makes the deer to give birth. His thunderbolt voice lays the forest bare. In his temple all fall before him with each one shouting, "Glory, glory, the God of glory!" Above the furious flood, the Enthroned One reigns, the King-God rules with eternity at his side. This is the one who gives his strength and might to his people. This is the Lord giving us his kiss of peace (Psalm 29:1-11 TPT).

There are a number of truths revealed in the above verses of Psalm 29 that Christians must acknowledge and in which Christians must actively begin to participate. Christians must concentrate on the *beauty of holiness of* the Lord. It is essential that Christians begin to fully grasp some basic characteristics of the Commander of angel armies. Please meditate upon the following eight items listed in Psalms often. The assignments of every Christian upon this earth are full of destiny and power. Those assignments include working with angels in this present and final move of God. Here are eight very important briefings from Psalm 29:

1. **Briefing one: Proclaim His majesty.**

   - All you mighty champions.

   - You sons of Almighty God.

   - Giving all the glory and strength back to Him!

2. **Briefing two: Be in awe before His majesty.**

   - Be in awe before such power and might!

   - Come worship wonderful Yahweh, arrayed in all His splendor.

   - Bow in worship as He appears in all His holy beauty.

   - Give Him the honor due His name.

   - Worship Him wearing the glory-garments of your holy, priestly calling!

3. **Briefing three: The voice of the Lord echoes through the skies and seas.**

   - The glory...God reigns as He thunders in the clouds.

   - So powerful is His voice, so brilliant and bright.

- How majestic is God as He thunders over the great waters!

- His tympanic thunder topples the strongest of trees.

- His symphonic sound splinters the mighty forests.

- Now He moves Zion's mountains by the might of His voice.

- He is shaking the snowy peaks with His earsplitting sound!

- The lightning-fire flashes, striking as He speaks.

- God reveals Himself when He makes the fault lines quake.

- He is shaking deserts, speaking His voice.

- God's mighty voice makes the deer to give birth.

- His thunderbolt voice lays the forest bare.

4. **Briefing four: In His temple all fall before Him with each one shouting "Glory, glory, the God of glory!"**

5. **Briefing five: Above the furious flood, the Enthroned One reigns.**

6. **Briefing six: The King-God rules with eternity at His side.**

7. **Briefing seven: This is the One who gives His strength and might to His people.**

8. **Briefing eight: This is the Lord giving us His kiss of peace.**

In briefing one, *proclaim His majesty*, we must rightfully discern the high rank and authority of our King. When you are in the presence of the King of all kings, you will worship Him and give Him credit for everything that He has done. We are sons and daughters of the most High God. We stand along with the angels who are our fellow servants. Angels are sometimes referred to as sons of God in the Scriptures. "Now there was a day when the sons of God came to present themselves before the Lord, and Satan also came among them" (Job 1:6).

After Christians have proclaimed His majesty, they should remember that His children are addressed in the Scripture verses as *mighty champions*. Every Christian is a child of the Most High God, and therefore every Christian has a wonderful inheritance. God also calls Christians mighty champions. The effectiveness of every believer in this last move is greatly enhanced as Christians stand with the angels. Angels also are mighty champions. Referring to Christians in this manner influences their effectiveness in the earth. As Christians yield to the Lord, acknowledging the strength and the glory to Him who sits on the throne, each one becomes able to be a champion. This move of God will become mighty, and Christians will always acknowledge that God is the One who ultimately will receive all the credit for victories.

In briefing two, *be in awe before his majesty*, Christians must recognize the power and might of our God, Commander of angel armies. The revelation of how awesome and wonderful is our God will cause Christians to bow down and worship him. Engaging with God on this level causes believers to have much in common with the angels that surround every believer. Christians must come and see our wonderful God arrayed in the splendor of His holy beauty.

Now is the time to give the Lord the honor that His name deserves. Christians are to worship Him as priests of the Most High God. Christians must worship Him as the Scripture declares, and that means they must wear *glory garments* of the holy and priestly calling. Within this last great move of God, the calling upon Christians includes amazing exploits through the power of the Holy Spirit.

> *Out of the north comes golden splendor [and people can hardly look on it]; around God is awesome splendor and majesty [far too glorious for man's eyes]* (Job 37:22 AMP).

In briefing three, *the voice of the Lord echoes through the skies and seas*, the focus is upon the voice of the Lord God as it reverberates throughout creation. This is the same voice to which the angels hearken and obey constantly. And this is the same voice that speaks to believers. God's voice thunders like the clouds. The voice of the Lord is very powerful. He speaks truth, and He speaks the destiny of believers. Christians have a very bright future that is foretold as God's voice goes forth to accomplish that which God has spoken. God's voice influences the trees and the mountains. According to Scripture, as the Lord speaks lightning fire flashes, striking where He sends it. The same voice that causes earthquakes and thunder bolts is the same voices that says, "I love you and I have plans for you that will cause you to prosper." Remember, the same voice that gives commands to angels also gives commands to His children.

Briefing four tells us that *in His temple all fall before Him with each one shouting "Glory, glory, the God of glory!"* As believers begin to fall down and shout, "Glory!" over and over again, each person will see the many angels that surround them. They will notice that the angels are eager for God's children to join in the worship. When Christians step out in faith and bow and worship, they will discover that angels love to join them. Angels love to worship God with Christians. According to Romans 12:2, when a Christian glorifies God in his or her body, that act is a living sacrifice. It is essential that believers present themselves to God and give Him all the glory for everything, including life. When believers give God this recognition, then great things will begin to happen in each person's life. The angels know when Christians have been obedient to the Word of God. Angels duly note that true worship in the record books of Heaven. Angels record the sacrifice that Christians give to God in worship, and they record that sacrifice immediately as the worship goes forth.

> *Then those who feared the Lord spoke to one another, and the Lord listened and heard them; so a book of remembrance was written before Him for those who fear the Lord and who meditate on His name* (Malachi 3:16).

In briefing five we will discuss *above the furious flood, the Enthroned One reigns.* The truth that believers need to glean from this portion of Psalm 29, is this: the Commander of the Lord's army, "The Enthroned One," is reigning above all turmoil on the earth. No matter what happens here on earth in a believer's life, his or her Commander sits enthroned above it all! According to Psalm 91, God will give a command concerning a believer. He will tell the angels to lift up the person. Nothing catches Almighty God by surprise. He is always ready to act on behalf of His own. His angels are standing by at this very moment to execute justice.

In briefing six, *the King-God rules with eternity at His side.* This is another very important truth concerning the agenda of angels and the part a Christian must play in these end times. Our God inhabits eternity. He also dwells with the contrite and humble in heart.

> *For thus says the High and Lofty One who inhabits eternity, whose name is Holy: "I dwell in the high and holy place, with him who has a contrite and humble spirit, to revive the spirit of the humble, and to revive the heart of the contrite ones"* (Isaiah 57:15).

Our God is not ruled by eternity; rather, He rules with eternity at His side, assisting Him. Every law that God has ever created is a law that is under His direction and that He oversees. Christians must realize that we will live an endless life in which a believer cannot lose if he or she will follow the Holy Spirit and the Word of God in a complete relationship with the Father. Believers are not limited by this realm because our God rules from Heaven with eternity at his side!

Briefing seven reveals *the One who gives His strength and might to His people.* God gives His angels strength; they are energized by His Word. Christians are also energized by His Word as He speaks from Heaven about every believer's destiny. Christians also have the same power that rose Jesus from the dead. According to Romans 8:11, that same power that rose Christ from the dead dwells within every believer. Christians must stand firm in all the will of God.

Every believer must develop a relationship with the destiny of his or her life upon this earth. God will cause our enemies to be scattered.

Briefing eight, the end of Psalm 29, says *this is the Lord, giving us His kiss of peace.* God gives every believer a kiss of peace. The kiss is a sign of the integrity, wholeness, and complete fulfillment of God's love for His own. He has made a covenant with His children through the blood of Jesus, and that covenant is sealed with this kiss. Christians cannot fail because His love for every believer will never fail. The angels cannot fail either. The angels go forth as the Lord commands. They go forth to encourage and help Christians through every situation in these end times.

> *O worship the Lord in the beauty of holiness; tremble before and reverently fear Him, all the earth. Say among the nations that the Lord reigns; the world also is established, so that it cannot be moved; He shall judge and rule the people righteously and with justice* (Psalm 96:9-10 AMPC).

Chapter 6

WAITING ON THE LORD

I wait quietly before God, for my victory comes
from him. He alone is my rock and my salvation,
my fortress where I will never be shaken.
—PSALM 62:1-2 NLT

Waiting on God is one of the most important things that anyone can do. In our society, we are not willing to wait for anything. People expect everything to be instantaneous in order for it to be right. We have learned to push things and manipulate things in order to see results. We are taught to be aggressive because we seem to think that without being aggressive, nothing will get done. That is why most people experience brokenness and weakness before they have a breakthrough and victory in any situation. I have found that waiting on the Lord causes us to become humble and broken in His sight. Within the experiences where I have waited upon the Lord, I have encountered Him and His angels. In waiting upon the Lord, I have given the opportunity for the Word of God and the Spirit of God to have time to work together in unity. Waiting upon God has been well worth the time spent. Waiting upon the Lord gives the Lord time to orchestrate a holy explosion.

The revelation that one must wait upon God is not popular. The condition of our society now requires instantaneous delivery of a solution to every challenge. However, it is true that anyone who has been used of God in both the Bible as well as in history has had to learn the lesson that patience and waiting are often keys to finding a solution to every challenge.

> *For thus says the High and Lofty One who inhabits eternity, whose name is Holy: "I dwell in the high and holy place, with him who has a contrite and humble spirit, to revive the spirit of the humble, and to revive the heart of the contrite ones"* (Isaiah 57:15).

Being on the other side of eternity, present with the Lord, has changed my perspective concerning what is really important in this life. There are certain truths in the Bible that I no longer question. To me, it does not matter who tries to say things that are not true. And, to me, it does not matter what they say that is not true. I have had the truth revealed to me by the Spirit of Truth. It has come to me both in spoken and written form. To me, the Bible is obviously the truth. I see the plans and purposes for people's lives are often much greater than they could ever conceive. I know that each person I encounter in this life does not necessarily know the deep secrets that God has planned for each one unless he or she is willing to wait patiently upon the Lord.

WAITING: A LOST ART

There is a great move of God coming upon the earth, and it has already started. However, Christians must begin the lost art of patiently waiting upon the Lord. If anyone were aware of how quickly God could move in one's life, he or she would give Him ample time to prepare the good things that He desires to pour out into his or her life. At this present time, Christians should be in this season of waiting upon the Lord. Angels know much more about what is going on in the earth and heavens than almost every Christian. However, this should not be the case. Christians have the Holy Spirit, the Counselor on the inside, leading them into all truth. Therefore, Christians should be aware of what is happening, both on the earth and in the heavens.

Every Christian should be in synchronization with what the angels are doing in his or her life at this very moment. It is time for believers to wait upon the Lord, meditating upon His Word and allowing the Holy Spirit to bring revelation into their realm of understanding. It is now time to realize that God has sealed plans and purposes for every believer. Those plans and purposes were written long before he or she was born. There are many examples in the Bible that show that God had chosen people to be deliverers of their generation. There are many prophetic voices in the world today. Christians who are reading this book right now are being activated into the destiny God has for this generation. Each person was brought into the Kingdom for such a time as this. It is obvious that angels are excited for what is about to happen in Christians' lives as they begin to follow divine destiny. It is time for every Christian to move into what God has ordained for his or her life.

MOSES WANTED MORE

Moses was chosen a man. He was called to be a great deliverer for Israel. He was to deliver Israel from bondage. He discerned that there was more to God than he knew. God told Moses that His presence would go with him. God told Moses that he would receive rest. But that was not all that God had for Moses. He recognized that God was holding something back from him and so he asked God to show him His glory. Here is the story:

> Then Moses said to the Lord, "See, You say to me, 'Bring up this people.' But You have not let me know whom You will send with me. Yet You have said, 'I know you by name, and you have also found grace in My sight.' Now therefore, I pray, if I have found grace in Your sight, show me now Your way, that I may know You and that I may find grace in Your sight. And consider that this nation is Your people." And He said, "My Presence will go with you, and I will give you rest."
>
> Then he said to Him, "If Your Presence does not go with us, do not bring us up from here. For how then will it be known that Your people and I have found grace in Your sight, except You go with us? So we shall

be separate, Your people and I, from all the people who are upon the face of the earth."

So the Lord said to Moses, "I will also do this thing that you have spoken; for you have found grace in My sight, and I know you by name." And he said, "Please, show me Your glory."

Then He said, "I will make all My goodness pass before you, and I will proclaim the name of the Lord before you. I will be gracious to whom I will be gracious, and I will have compassion on whom I will have compassion." But He said, "You cannot see My face; for no man shall see Me, and live." And the Lord said, "Here is a place by Me, and you shall stand on the rock. So it shall be, while My glory passes by, that I will put you in the cleft of the rock, and will cover you with My hand while I pass by. Then I will take away My hand, and you shall see My back; but My face shall not be seen" (Exodus 33:12-23).

One of the amazing things that happened to Moses was in the cleft of the rock. Moses was able to hear God speak His holy name. He also heard God describe Himself in a way that no one had ever heard before that time. When God passed by in all His goodness, He revealed who He is as a person. Moses found out that He is a good God who has compassion on whomever He desires to have compassion. Essentially, Moses had the revelation that God can do what He wants, when He wants, and to whom He wants.

ILLUMINATION

An amazing thing happens when we *wait upon the Lord*. As believers meditate upon His Word and allow the Spirit of God to bring forth truth from their spirits into their understanding, spiritually, they start to light up the spiritual atmosphere surrounding them. This will happen more and more as the days go by. It will happen more and more frequently because the time for the sons of God to be revealed is drawing closer. The atmosphere of Heaven is all around believers, and every Christian must have a spirit that is white hot with the Word of God and with Holy Ghost fire.

Soon, everything that the Lord has promised to every believer will come forth. It is time for every Christian to move and inherit the land the Lord has provided. Every Christian must wait upon Him and allow the Holy Spirit to ignite them from within. The angels will help every believer as the Holy Spirit ignites each person.

> *Wait on the Lord, and keep His way, and He shall exalt you to inherit the land* (Psalm 37:34).

The Lord wants to show each of His children His way of doing things. He wants to reveal His personality to every believer. He loves every Christian and is watching over them. His plans and purposes will definitely come to pass.

> *But it is wrong to say God doesn't listen, to say the Almighty isn't concerned. You say you can't see him, but he will bring justice if you will only **wait*** (Job 35:13-14 NLT).

Whatever a Christian may desire of the Lord, God desires to give him or her. As Christians wait upon the Lord, He will start to reveal His love to every person. The revelation will cause a quickening and an illumination in each believer's spirit. "Hear my voice according to Your steadfast love; O Lord, quicken me and give me life according to Your [righteous] decrees" (Ps. 119:149 AMPC).

JESUS IS WAITING

I remember waking up in my bedroom not long ago and seeing an angel that was standing across the room by the dresser. He was dressed differently than I have ever seen an angel dressed before that time. He stood before me, clothed in a very ornamented robe. It seemed as though he was waiting for me to wake up as he stood there. We were immediately caught up in the spirit. The angel took me to a specific place because he wanted to show me the secret of *waiting on God.*

I was shown the future. What I saw concerned the move of God that is coming to the earth. It was a move of the glory of the Father that saturated the atmosphere in the churches where I would be sent to preach. The angel told me that the time that I spend waiting on God will be in relation to the amount of the glory that I will be able to access in the ministry of the Holy Spirit. The angel was given permission to show me all these things so that I would be encouraged to *wait upon the Lord.* This possibility of being able to access a great amount of glory was going to be available in all the churches where I would go. I was shown churches where I had not yet even ministered. The Lord showed me that the glory was on the earth. He said Christians can enter into the glory by waiting upon Him.

Then, the angel took me into a room. Jesus was standing in that room, waiting for us. Jesus seemed sad because He said, "My people were not waiting upon Me." He wanted to teach me how important it is to wait in the presence of the Lord. I realized that when I wait upon the Lord, the glory will begin to increase in my life and ministry. Next, the door through which we had just walked closed. The space that we occupied became an elevator.

Within the space, there were buttons to display the different levels of revelation that we could attain as we waited upon the Lord. The space was actually a *room of waiting*. I asked Jesus which floor I should choose, and He said that the floor that I chose was up to me. He asked me, "How long do you want to wait upon Me?" He bowed His head, and so did the angel. I bowed my head, and we waited. I felt the whole room start to ascend into the glory realm. After a while, I looked up. The elevator stopped climbing, and the door opened up. We had ascended to a really high place. The room was full of the revelation knowledge and glory of God.

As I looked out the door, I was looking down and seeing my life as God sees it. We had gone so high that all the things that troubled me were so small. This was the result of waiting on God. Jesus had taken me to His vantage point. It was a much better perspective of my life than I had previously known before I waited upon Him in the room of revelation.

Every Christian must receive Heaven's perspective for his or her life. This angel was given permission to show me that it is exceedingly important to wait upon God. The amount of time that a Christian is willing to wait upon the Lord is directly related to the amount of the glory God will reveal in this generation.

So the Lord must wait for you to come to him so he can show you his love and compassion. For the Lord is a faithful God. Blessed are those who wait for his help (Isaiah 30:18 NLT).

THE KEY

The move of God is under way in this generation. The key is not to forcefully pursue His revelation and glory by soulish manipulation. The key here is but to *wait upon the Lord.* He will cause a great and mighty flow of the glory. There are many things that must be revealed to every Christian so that he or she is able to understand the specific and unique ministry that God has given to him or her as a believer. It is especially important at this time in history for each Christian to wait upon the Lord. The angels have been assigned to every Christian to make sure that each one can receive all the briefings from Heaven that are needed in this time for this generation. I know that each believer desires to be faithful to God. Just remember, the angels of Heaven are assigned to each believer, and their desire is for each believer to be faithful to God as well. Angels are trained agents of faithfulness. They cannot be denied if a Christian will continue trusting God and let angels do their job.

Believers are chosen as beloved children who have a destiny and a bright future. Every believer needs to grasp, by the Spirit's revelation, who he or she is to Father God. The apostle Paul said this well about our future glory:

Yet what we suffer now is nothing compared to the glory he will reveal to us later. For all creation is waiting eagerly for that future day when God will reveal who his children really are. Against its will, all creation was subjected to God's curse. But with eager hope, the creation looks forward to the day when it will join God's children in glorious freedom from death and decay. For we know that all creation has been groaning as in the pains of childbirth right up to the present time. And we believers also groan, even though we have the Holy Spirit within us as a foretaste of future glory, for we long for our bodies to be released from sin and suffering. We, too, wait with eager hope for the day when God will give us our full rights as his adopted children, including the new bodies he has promised us. We were given this hope when we were saved. (If we already have something, we don't need to hope for it. But if we look forward to something we don't yet have, we must wait patiently and confidently) (Romans 8:18-25 NLT).

IT IS TIME TO RISE UP AS GOD'S BELOVED CHILD. YOUR FATHER IS COMING TO VISIT YOU IN ALL OF HIS GLORY. HE WANTS YOU TO KNOW HIM IN A MORE INTIMATE WAY. HE WANTS TO PASS BY YOU AND SHOW YOU WHO HE IS. THE ANGELS HAVE BROUGHT YOU TO THIS PLACE THAT IS SO SACRED. IT IS A PLACE OF REVELATION, AND IT IS A PLACE OF WAITING UPON THE LORD. HIS SPECIAL DESTINY FOR YOU WILL BE REVEALED.

Chapter 7

THE GLORY OF THE LORD HAS COME

And it came to pass, when the priests came out of the holy place, that the cloud filled the house of the Lord, so that the priests could not continue ministering because of the cloud; for the glory of the Lord filled the house of the Lord.
—1 KINGS 8:10-11

The glory of the Lord is such a powerful thing in these last days. The words of Jesus reveal that the glory of God originated with the Father. The glory has been shared with the Son throughout eternity.

The Spirit of God will reveal the glory of the Lord in these last days as the move of God comes forth.

THE TIMELESS PAST

Before the foundation of the world was laid, Jesus Christ was with the Father God, the great Jehovah, in the *timeless past*. They, together with the mighty Holy Spirit, rule and reign in a Kingdom that has no beginning and no end because time and distance do not exist in God's Kingdom. Living in the realms that have none of the familiar boundaries to which people are accustomed on the earth, all limitations are completely removed. Human beings on earth follow reference points that seem as if they follow a timeline. People fulfill commitments based on the clock, calendar, and the distance traveled. These three things—clock, calendar, and distance—are all centered upon the speed at which we can accomplish tasks in a timely manner. If we can travel at high speed, then our day can accommodate more events. These are limitations found within our earthly realm.

What are some of the limitations that everyone experiences in life? Christians must rely upon God who lives in glory to remove the limitations that generally face everyone on earth. Angels sent to help Christians have beheld the glory of the Father. Christians can learn how to operate in the glory so that the limitations of this world are removed. Jesus prayed the following prayer to help His own experience God's glory:

> *This is what Jesus prayed as he looked up into heaven, "Father, the time has come. Unveil the glorious splendor of your Son so that I will magnify your glory! You have already given me authority over all people*

126

so that I may give the gift of eternal life to all those that you have given to me. Eternal life means to know and experience you as the only true God, and to know and experience Jesus Christ, as the Son whom you have sent. I have glorified you on the earth by faithfully doing everything you've told me to do. So my Father, restore me back to the glory that we shared together when we were face-to-face before the universe was created" (John 17:1-5 TPT).

This passage of Scripture reveals that Jesus was clearly with the Father in glory from the beginning. Jesus has announced that the glory of the Lord has been revealed by the ministry that He accomplished. Jesus asked to be returned to the rightful place that He occupied with His Father from the beginning. It is amazing that Jesus claims to have been given the authority over the people and that He has the authority to give them the gift of eternal life. This gift includes the experience of knowing God Himself. Now Jesus is back, face to face with the Father. This was the way things were organized before the universe was even created.

Mankind's thinking has been limited because it is based upon false teaching and wrong perceptions. Christians need to renew their minds. They must recognize an eternal life that has always existed. Believers can enter into this realm if they allow their minds to be renewed. After renewing their minds, Christians are then able to understand the things of God. Renewing of the mind will help Christians be ready to actively participate in the last move of God. This final move of the Lord includes the glory realm. In the spirit, limitations have been removed. Believers will still be limited if their minds are not renewed. And Christians will still be limited by our bodies, which have not yet been redeemed. So minds must be renewed and bodies must be redeemed to remove the limitations and free Christians to participate in the new things of God that will include His glory revealed.

SURRENDERED LIVES

Jesus says that the Father has placed all people under His authority. When Jesus accomplished the tasks of revealing the Father to the world and redeeming mankind, He said the following profound statement: "For all who belong to me now belong to you. And all who belong to you now belong to me as well, and my glory is revealed through their surrendered lives" (John 17:10 TPT).

So Jesus says that the glory of the Father that was given to Him can be revealed in believers. That glory is revealed through Christians' lives when they are fully surrendered to the Lord. Therefore, if Christians will continue to surrender their lives to God and to the divine purpose for which He has called them in this generation, the glory of the Father will be revealed through His children. Christians are redeemed by the blood of Jesus. The purpose and plan of God is for Jesus's ministry to be carried out on the earth through all believers. Jesus wanted Christians to do greater works than He.

> *Most assuredly, I say to you, he who believes in Me, the works that I do he will do also; and greater works than these he will do, because I go to My Father. And whatever you ask in My name, that I will do, that the Father may be glorified in the Son. If you ask anything in My name, I will do it* (John 14:12-14).

The very works that Jesus did on the earth gave evidence that the Father has shared the glory with His Son. Jesus said:

> *Most assuredly, I say to you, the Son can do nothing of Himself, but what He sees the Father do; for whatever He does, the Son also does in like manner. For the Father loves the Son, and shows Him all things that He Himself does; and He will show Him greater works than these, that you may marvel. For as the Father raises the dead and gives life to them, even so the Son gives life to whom He will* (John 5:19-21).

GREATER WORKS

Christians with surrendered lives can experience the glory of the Father. Christians must ask themselves, "Are you ready?" I know that the Holy Spirit and the angels are ready to have the glory of the Lord revealed on the earth! Jesus transferred ownership of the people to His Father. Christians must totally commit their lives to the Father. When they are fully committed, the authority and power to do the same works that Jesus did becomes available to Christians. The works that Jesus did glorified the Father, and now Christians have the opportunity to also do works that glorify the Father. Jesus said that believers will do greater works than even He did, so they should be prepared to encounter greater glory. God the Father desires to be involved in this present move of the Spirit, where His authority and power bring great glory to the earth. As Christians surrender their lives, the glory of the Father will be revealed, and the Father will be able to do mighty works through us. Those mighty works will be unlimited because God has removed the limitations that mankind normally meets.

And these signs will follow those who believe: In My name they will cast out demons; they will speak with new tongues; they will take up serpents; and if they drink anything deadly, it will by no means hurt them; they will lay hands on the sick, and they will recover (Mark 16:17-18).

The signs that follow believers will glorify the Father. Believers must yield to the glory. Jesus wants us to share in the same glory that He shares with the Father. The Father loves Christians just as He loves Jesus. We need to renew our minds to this very truth. The prayer that Jesus prayed for all who would believe in Him is within John 17. That prayer contains several important principles that Christians need to know. Believers must begin to realize who they are in Christ and what has already been done for them. When Christians start to understand this, then they can begin to enjoy the realm of the glory that is coming to the earth with this next great and final move of the Lord upon the earth. One must understand the glory realm in order to operate with angels. Angels help bring the glory of the Father to the earth. This great move will reveal the Father's love and personality.

JESUS PRAYS FOR YOU

We must recognize that all of the prayers of Jesus are always answered. Jesus prays for every Christian. Therefore, every Christian can rest assured that the Father will answer the prayers Jesus prays for His own. Jesus prays for every Christian, and His prayers make it possible that every one of them can experience the glory of God and the love of God in the same manner in which Jesus experiences the glory of God and the love of God.

And I ask not only for these disciples, but also for all those who will one day believe in me through their message. I pray for them all to be joined together as one even as you and I, Father, are joined together as one. I pray for them to become one with us so that the world will recognize that you sent me. For the very glory you have given to me I have given them so that they will be joined together as one and experience the same unity that we enjoy. You live fully in me and now I live fully in them so that they will experience perfect unity, and the world will be convinced that you have sent me, for they will see that you love each one of them with the same passionate love that you have for me. Father, I ask that you allow everyone that you have given to me to be with me where I am! Then they will see my full glory—the very splendor you have placed upon me because you have loved me even before the beginning of time (John 17:20-24 TPT).

In John 17, there are some important verses that every Christian must understand. This important information has to do with the glory of the Lord. Every Christian's assignments on this earth are powerful, and every Christian must have an understanding of the glory of the Lord to fulfill his or her destiny upon the earth. In addition, every Christian's assignments on this earth include working with angels in the glory.

There are six very important briefings that Christians need to understand to assist God. Christians have a part in helping God on the earth today. John 17 highlights the following principles:

1.   **Briefing one: I pray for them all to be joined together as one.**

     - Even as you and I, Father, are joined together as one.

2.   **Briefing two: I pray for them to become one with us.**

     - So that the world will recognize that you sent me.

3.   **Briefing three: For the very glory you have given to me I have given them.**

     - So that they will be joined together as one.
     - And experience the same unity that we enjoy.

4.   **Briefing four: You live fully in me and now I live fully in them.**

     - So that they will experience perfect unity.

5.   **Briefing five: The world will be convinced that you have sent me.**

     - For they will see that you love each one of them.
     - With the same passionate love that you have for me.

6.   **Briefing six: Father, I ask that you allow everyone that you have given to me to be with me where I am!**

- Then they will see my full glory.

- The very splendor you have placed upon me.

- Because you have loved me even before the beginning of time.

In briefing one, *I pray for them all to be joined together as one,* Jesus profoundly prays for us to be joined together in unity. In the glory, there must be unity and agreement. Believers live in the most opportune and amazing time. They have the opportunity to work with angels in the glory of the Father. Jesus will receive the answer to His prayer for unity amongst believers. The unity of the believers will be just as great as the unity that Jesus and the Father share with one another. Believers will work as one in these last days, and the prayers of Jesus for unity amongst the believers will be answered. When Christians move together in unity, their prayers cannot be denied. We shall be given everything for which we ask. There will be great unity for us in the Godhead in this final move of the Lord upon the earth.

In briefing two, *I pray for them to become one with Us,* Christians realize that the Father has truly restored His own to Himself through Jesus Christ. The Father wants every Christian to be with Him. He desires that every Christian partake in those things which He is doing on the earth. The greater works that Christians will do are about to come forth. The world is going to know that believers have been sent by God. The world will recognize Jesus as the Name above all names. At that Name, every knee will bow. The apostle Paul said:

> *At the name of Jesus every knee should bow, of those in heaven, and of those on earth, and of those under the earth, and that every tongue should confess that*

Jesus Christ is Lord, to the glory of God the Father (Philippians 2:10-11).

Briefing three, *for the very glory You have given to Me I have given them,* is one of the most profound statements Jesus has ever spoken. We have been given the same glory as Jesus. We are sharing in the glory of God as a gift from Jesus. The glory of God is the in the same realm as the glory with angels. Christians, God, and the angels join together as one. Believers are able to experience the same unity that Jesus and the Father enjoy. It will be unbelievable when Christians, God, and the angels are in unity with no resistance. Angels are going to be full of joy because the job they have to do will be much easier when complete unity arrives. There will be unity in the faith, as well as unity in the fear of the Lord. The glory of God will increase greatly, and much joy will abound!

Briefing four, *You live fully in Me and now I live fully in them,* states things similarly to John 15 because it presents two similar ideas—abiding in Christ and abiding in the Vine. Abiding in the Vine is a process that takes time to develop. There is a mighty river of life flowing from the throne of God. That river of life will spring up in Christians, causing them to walk in the supernatural in these last days. The Holy Spirit will spring up as a river from the bellies, the Spirit within, of God's people. Things of the supernatural are going to come forth more and more easily as Christians experience the full unity of the Godhead flowing through themselves in the glory realm.

Briefing five, *the world will be convinced that You have sent Me,* is an amazing truth that will happen. When a person is able to experience the glory of the Father, unity will bring the love of God into Christians' lives. That love will overflow from each one to others. People must be loved and experience perfect love before they are actually able to love. New revelation of the Father's love is going to occur in this last great move of God. Christians will learn to love each other. We will have the revelation of how much the Father loves us. That love for one another will be a passionate, brotherly love. Christians will begin to understand that they have become irresistible to God the Father through Jesus Christ. Believers will begin to understand that God is pursuing them. When Christians become fully convinced that Jesus was sent from the Father and loves us, the world will be convinced as well. Many people will come to know the Lord during this final and great move of the glory. The angels will be ready to bring in the harvest. They will have great joy, knowing that the harvest will populate Heaven.

The last is briefing six: *Father, I ask that You allow everyone that You have given to Me to be with Me where I am!* Jesus asks the Father to allow Him to bring us to abide with Him. When Christians see Jesus in His full glory, then they will understand why Jesus wants everyone to know that He has asked the Father to allow believers to be with Him. The glory of the Father is very bright. It is actually difficult to see in such glory. The bright splendor displayed has to do with the Father's love. Jesus is engulfed in this splendor of love. Christians will be like Him, and they will experience this splendor also. Believers will be encouraged because they will begin to recognize that the glory of God is presently here.

> You ask, "Who is this King of Glory?" He is the Lord of Victory, armed and ready for battle, the Mighty One, the invincible commander of heaven's hosts! Yes, he is the King of Glory! Pause in his presence (Psalm 24:10 TPT).

DAZZLING GLORY

I remember encountering the dazzling glory of the throne room and of Heaven. I have been to the River of Life where the water appears as liquid diamonds and is full of eternal life. In Heaven, there is no sun, but the water is so bright and sparkling that I could not look at it directly sometimes. In Heaven, there is so much gold, so many other precious metals, and so many precious stones, that everything just sparkles. Everything is so clean in Heaven. That is because the *fear of the Lord* is there in Heaven. Heaven is God's home, and He has invited Christians to live with Him. "Lord, I love your home, this place of dazzling glory, bathed in the splendor and light of your presence!" (Ps. 26:8 TPT).

Paths of Integrity

The glory of Heaven's provision is available to every Christian. No Christian even has to ask for that provision. God has created Heaven so beautifully. No one who goes to Heaven ever wants to leave and come back to earth. In Heaven, if one looks in the sky, one sees no sun because God is the brightness of Heaven's glory. The glory shines with sparkling splendor. If Christians choose to walk on the path with the Lord, they must choose to follow Him completely. Christians must be truthful with God and with themselves. They must also be truthful with our fellow man in the coming days. God will give us the grace to be truthful.

> *For the Lord God is brighter than the brilliance of a sunrise! Wrapping himself around me like a shield, he is so generous with his gifts of grace and glory. Those who walk along his paths with integrity will*

never lack one thing they need, for he provides it all!
(Psalm 84:11 TPT)

Trust

It is important to meditate on the fact that our God is head of the angel armies. God faithfully executes His desires to the believers upon the earth. The angels serve Him to help every Christian. The children of God need not have worries or concerns. Christians can completely trust the Lord. "O Lord of Heaven's Armies, what euphoria fills those who forever trust in you!" (Ps. 84:12 TPT).

Endless Glory

Our Father God lives forever. Therefore, God also has an endless reign of power. When a Christian approaches God, he or she must approach the Father in the glory. God is ruling from the highest position in the universe. His reign will never end. We are secure in Him. "But you, O Lord, are exalted forever in the highest place of endless glory" (Ps. 92:8 TPT).

Tied to the Alter

God recognizes that worship creates a sacred and holy place. God loves altars, and He loves sacrifices as well. Christians can continually offer themselves on the altar of God as a living sacrifice, just as it says in Romans 12:2. As the glory flows into the church, believers will spend extended times at the altar in repentance and worship. The psalmist says, "For the Lord our God has brought us his glory-light. I offer him my life in joyous sacrifice. Tied tightly to your altar I will bring you praise. For you are the God of my life and I lift you high, exalting you to the highest place" (Ps. 118:27 TPT). It is time for every Christian to fully give himself or herself to God and to be joined to the altar of God permanently. The Lord expects

His children to have that full commitment to Him as we enter into this glorious time of the Father's revelation. He will show His own who He really is in this next great and final move of God.

Former Glory

We know about the present move of God and the revelation of His glory. His angels are already here to assist every believer in this new and final move of God. As the psalmist says, this is to be the prayer of Christians: "Now, Lord, do it again! Restore us to our former glory! May streams of your refreshing flow over us until our dry hearts are drenched again" (Ps. 126:4 TPT).

Sincere Humility

The glory realm of God the Father has no room for pride. Christians must humble themselves before our mighty God and surrender completely to Him. As soon as Christians repent fully, we will have unity in the Spirit corporately, and the Shekinah glory will be revealed.

> *The source of revelation-knowledge is found as you fall down in surrender before the Lord. Don't expect to see Shekinah glory until the Lord sees your sincere humility* (Proverbs 15:33 TPT).

The Veil Is Lifted

The glory realm will increase more and more, and the angels will be present in every service, rejoicing as the unsaved come to hear the Word of God. Christians must realize that the unsaved come to God's meetings to hear the message of the gospel. Angels rejoice in the harvest as they see those who will be saved, healed, and delivered. Those who have not been able to see the truth of the gospel and those who have been blind to the things of God will have their spiritual eyes opened. They will begin to receive the Good News of God as the truth. It is time for believers to become aware that a full relationship with Christ and the love of the Father are available. Very soon, believers will be translated into the glory of God.

> *But the moment one turns to the Lord with an open heart, the veil is lifted and they see. Now, the "Lord" I'm referring to is the Holy Spirit, and wherever he is Lord, there is freedom. We can all draw close to him with the veil removed from our faces. And with no veil we all become like mirrors who brightly reflect the glory of the Lord Jesus. We are being transfigured into his very image as we move from one brighter level of glory to another. And this glorious transfiguration comes from the Lord, who is the Spirit* (2 Corinthians 3:16-18 TPT).

Set Times

The heavenly realms are touching the physical realm of earth through the ministry of the Holy Spirit. The Holy Spirit works through believers everywhere. As Christians continue to intercede and pray, they will see God's timetable revealed. The seasons have already shifted. The angels are already on their missions for this final move. Believers do not have to fully understand everything that is happening in order to participate in this great and final move of the Lord. Christians have been filled with the spirit of power and been given all the tools that are necessary to bring in the harvest in this time of glory.

> *He answered, "The Father is the one who sets the fixed dates and the times of their fulfillment. You*

are not permitted to know the timing of all that he has prepared by his own authority. But I promise you this—the Holy Spirit will come upon you and you will be filled with power. And you will be my messengers to Jerusalem, throughout Judea, the distant provinces—even to the remotest places on earth! (Acts 1:7-8 TPT)

Chapter 8

THE WORD OF THE LORD

*As for God, His way is perfect; the word of the Lord
is proven; He is a shield to all who trust in Him .*
—PSALM 18:30

There is a prophetic word that comes to every generation. That word of prophecy is a glimpse into the mind and will of God. It is revealed for the benefit of all involved. Some will not heed the word, and therefore they will encounter the consequences of their disobedience. The Almighty God is righteous. He is just in every way. He will judge fairly in every case. Thankfully, we who hear and receive the gospel message have heeded the word and have escaped the curse, eternal death, and every evil thing. When there is a prophetic word that goes forth, God is saying something to produce an expected end. "For I know the thoughts that I think toward you, says the Lord, thoughts of peace and not of evil, to give you a future and a hope" (Jer. 29:11).

At the end of this age, God has spoken to us in many ways. He has laid a strong foundation of truth by His word. Then, as the Book of Hebrews says, He has spoken to us by His Son in these last days.

In many separate revelations [each of which set forth a portion of the Truth] and in different ways God spoke of old to [our] forefathers in and by the prophets, [but] in the last of these days He has spoken to us in [the person of a] Son, Whom He appointed Heir and lawful Owner of all things, also by and through Whom He created the worlds and the reaches of space and the ages of time [He made, produced, built, operated, and arranged them in order]. He is the sole expression of the glory of God [the Light-being, the out-raying or radiance of the divine], and He is the perfect imprint and very image of [God's] nature, upholding and maintaining and guiding and propelling the universe by His mighty word of power. When He had by offering Himself accomplished our cleansing of sins and riddance of guilt, He sat down at the right hand of the divine Majesty on high, [taking a place and rank by which] He Himself became as

much superior to angels as the glorious Name (title)
which He has inherited is different from and more
excellent than theirs (Hebrews 1:1-4 AMPC).

The Lord wants to speak to this generation in a profound way. Any time that God speaks, it is *absolute truth*. God's intention for any word that He gives is always preemptive. The Lord's intention for the word is also always looking toward the future. He delivers truth to the people in due time so they can deal with things promptly. He provides His truth so that judgment does not have to occur. God answers a previous generation's prayers. This generation receives benefit from those prayers. God is calling this present generation back to its first love. When a generation has strayed from its first love, God must use His Word to call them back to that love. Remember this important point: At times, a prophetic word goes forth to a people who do not yet perceive the need that they have for that particular word.

YOUR FIRST LOVE

Jesus desires that this generation will to return to their first love. Our heavenly Father wants the Spirit of God to have His way in our own personal lives, as well as in the corporate church setting. He longs for deep fellowship with His people. One evening years ago in my office in Phoenix, Arizona, the Lord asked me this question: "Why did I ask the apostle John to write letters to the seven pastors of the seven churches in the Book of Revelation?" I told the Lord that I did not know why John wrote those letters. The Lord said to me, "I told John to write the letters because those seven pastors were not listening to Me, so I had to reach them through John." I did not expect this conversation with God, and it took me by surprise.

Until the Lord spoke these words to me, I had mistakenly thought that everyone in leadership would hear Jesus's voice for themselves.

As I began to study men and women of God throughout different generations, including those who have been involved in various moves of God throughout the ages, I realized that, for the most part, they were not always accepted by the mainstream church community. Those who participated in a supernatural lifestyle were oftentimes ridiculed and left out of the mainstream religion of their generation. These people were only celebrated as heroes of faith in the next generation. Even Jesus Himself was hated by the established religion of the day. Jesus was killed by them. And now Jesus has been exalted to the highest place in Heaven and given a Name that is above all names. Almost every apostle was killed for his supernatural lifestyle by his own generation, only to be celebrated by the following generations as heroes of the faith.

It is no different for prophets who speak the word of the Lord to a generation. They are ridiculed, ignored, and some of these men and women have even been killed for speaking forth the word of the Lord. They suffer, only to be celebrated in the following generations. Jesus said:

> *Great sorrow awaits you religious scholars and Pharisees—frauds and imposters! You build memorials for the prophets your ancestors killed and decorate the monuments of the godly people your ancestors murdered. Then you boast, "If we had lived back then, we would never have permitted them to kill the prophets." But your words and deeds testify that you are just like them and prove that you are indeed the descendants of those who murdered the prophets. Go*

ahead and finish what your ancestors started! You are nothing but snakes in the grass, the offspring of poisonous vipers! How will you escape the judgment of hell if you refuse to turn in repentance? For this reason I will send you more prophets and wise men and teachers of truth. Some you will crucify, and some you will beat mercilessly with whips in your meeting houses, abusing and persecuting them from city to city. As your penalty, you will be held responsible for the righteous blood spilled and the murders of every godly person throughout your history—from the blood of righteous Abel to the blood of Zechariah, son of Jehoiada, whom you killed as he stood in the temple between the brazen altar and the Holy Place. I tell you the truth: the judgment for all these things will fall upon this generation! (Matthew 23:29-36 TPT)

I asked Jesus what I should say to this generation when I realized that He was going to send me back to life on earth. After I had been with Him in Heaven, I returned to earth with an understanding concerning my generation—they did not know that they had strayed from their First Love. I did not know what to say to this generation. It is difficult to explain to them that they have left their first love. And the fact that they are unaware that they have left their first love makes the explanation that I have to give them even more difficult to deliver. It is a challenge to figure out a way to speak to people and cause them to see their need to return to their first love, especially when they have not yet even realized that they have left their first love.

Simply put, the *Word of the Lord* is a clarion call for God's people. Many Christians today are a "fatherless generation" in their experience in this life. They lack the relationship with the heavenly Father. They fail to live in close relationship with a God who loves them dearly. If a person does not have any experience with an earthly father who loves him or her dearly, that very person may find it difficult to accept love from a heavenly Father whom one cannot see. But our Lord has thought of every one of us. He has breathed life into each of our lives, placed every one of us into our mother's womb, and written a book about every one of us before one day of any of our lives ever came to pass (see Ps. 139).

The Word of the Lord came to John concerning one of the seven churches in the Book of Revelation. That particular church had become lukewarm toward the things of God. Jesus addressed that church in a letter that was written by John. The church did not know they were lukewarm. In fact, they were not aware that they were in any kind of need at the time. So the Word of the Lord came to inform them of their need, even though they did not perceive it. The Laodiceans were not asking for help, despite the fact that they desperately needed God's help.

> *And to the angel of the church of the Laodiceans write, "These things says the Amen, the Faithful and True Witness, the Beginning of the creation of God: 'I know your works, that you are neither cold nor hot. I could wish you were cold or hot. So then, because you are lukewarm, and neither cold nor hot, I will vomit you out of My mouth. Because you say, "I am rich, have become wealthy, and have need of nothing"—and do not know that you are wretched, miserable, poor, blind, and naked— I counsel you to buy from Me gold refined in the fire, that you may be rich; and white garments, that you may be clothed,*

that the shame of your nakedness may not be revealed; and anoint your eyes with eye salve, that you may see. As many as I love, I rebuke and chasten. Therefore be zealous and repent. Behold, I stand at the door and knock. If anyone hears My voice and opens the door, I will come in to him and dine with him, and he with Me. To him who overcomes I will grant to sit with Me on My throne, as I also overcame and sat down with My Father on His throne. He who has an ear, let him hear what the Spirit says to the churches' (Revelation 3:14-22).

PATHWAYS TO THE NEXT MOVE

There are certain pathways that God chooses in every generation to usher in a mighty move of God's Spirit. If one studies how things began for the church in the Book of Acts, one will, perhaps, better perceive and understand the ways of God. The believers were told to wait in Jerusalem for power from on high. On the day of Pentecost, they were together in unity, which is a supernatural event in itself. Unity is a key to the beginning and continuing of any great move of God. They were in one accord. The second supernatural sign that followed that unity was the sound of a mighty, rushing wind. The third supernatural sign was the appearance of Holy Spirit fire upon the head of every believer. The fourth supernatural sign was each believer speaking in other languages. These languages were spoken by believers who had never spoken those languages previously, and who had never been taught those languages. The fifth and final supernatural sign was the believers so filled with of the Spirit of God that each appeared to be drunk during the afternoon.

When the Day of Pentecost had fully come, they were all with one accord in one place. And suddenly there came a sound from heaven, as of a rushing mighty wind, and it filled the whole house where they were sitting. Then there appeared to them divided tongues, as of fire, and one sat upon each of them. And they were all filled with the Holy Spirit and began to speak with other tongues, as the Spirit gave them utterance. ...Others mocking said, "They are full of new wine" (Acts 2:1-4,13).

To summarize, the body of Christ and the church began on that day, the Day of Pentecost, and what Christians experienced then were the following supernatural events:

1. Unity

2. Mighty rushing wind

3. Holy Ghost fire

4. Supernatural utterance/ tongues

5. Holy Spirit joy/drunkenness in the Spirit

So what has happened in the last 2,000 years that we have become so sophisticated now? Are we presently experiencing the same supernatural events as when the church first began?

Your new life in the Anointed One began with the Holy Spirit giving you a new birth. Why then would you so foolishly turn from living in the Spirit by trying to finish by your own works? (Galatians 3:3 TPT)

INGREDIENTS IN THE NEXT MOVE OF GOD

1. *The Fear of the Lord*

Discerning that the Lord is awesome in splendor and glory is the first step to understanding the fear of the Lord. He is holy beyond comprehension, and He has commanded us to be holy. First Peter 1:16 says, "You are to be holy, because I am holy" (TPT). The fear of the Lord is where we start, because Proverbs 9:10 says, "The fear of the Lord is the beginning of wisdom, and the knowledge of the Holy One is understanding."

2. *Repentance*

When a person has turned his or her face away from God and one's focus is not upon the Lord, there will be a gradual cooling down of one's spiritual life. Eventually, one becomes spiritually lukewarm. Repentance involves turning one's attention back to God by looking at Him face to face with no consciousness of sin. If a person's focus is not upon God completely, he or she must make the correct adjustments. Any time that one's focus is not upon the Lord, it is time to turn toward Him and pursue Him completely, with everything one possesses within himself or herself.

3. *Spiritual Hunger*

King David pursued God with everything within himself. Joshua sought God at every opportunity that he could. Joshua sought Him while he was in the tent of meeting. Jesus set Himself apart to pray in the mountains at night. When a person hungers and thirsts for righteousness, he or she will be filled (see Matt. 5:6). It is time to pursue God completely. He is a rewarder of those who diligently seek Him (see Heb. 11:6).

4. The Return of Holy Altars

It is time for each Christian to consecrate himself or herself completely at the altar of God in the church. We must seek Him corporately. Coming to an altar and presenting oneself to the Lord is not an old-fashioned act but a sacred act of worship. We are to present our bodies as a living sacrifice.

> *Beloved friends, what should be our proper response to God's marvelous mercies? I encourage you to surrender yourselves to God to be his sacred, living sacrifices. And live in holiness, experiencing all that delights his heart. For this becomes your genuine expression of worship* (Romans 12:1 TPT).

5. Brokenness/Humility

Every move of God sprang forth from a Christian's experience of brokenness and humility. He dwells with the humble and contrite heart. We must rid ourselves of all pride because James 4:6 says, "But He gives more grace. Therefore He says: 'God resists the proud, but gives grace to the humble.'"

6. The Crucified Life

The apostle Paul understood the crucified life and taught that "I have been crucified with Christ; it is no longer I who live, but Christ lives in me; and the life which I now live in the flesh I live by faith in the Son of God, who loved me and gave Himself for me" (Gal. 2:20). Jesus Himself told His disciples that they must deny themselves and carry their own cross to be His disciple (see Luke 9:23). The apostle Paul preached that we were to give no provision to the flesh (see Rom. 13:14).

7. *Deep Spiritual Worship*

When Christians learn to yield themselves to a deep spiritual worship that comes from the heavenly realms, they will enter into the glory cloud of Heaven. As believers join together in one voice in Heaven and on the earth, they will worship as one family and give the "One who sits on the throne" all the glory. They will signify who God is and what He has done by giving Him all the glory. Angels will join Christians as they worship the King of Kings.

MEDITATE ON PSALM 119

Aleph

Blessed are the undefiled in the way, who walk in the law of the Lord! Blessed are those who keep His testimonies, who seek Him with the whole heart! They also do no iniquity; they walk in His ways. You have commanded us to keep Your precepts diligently. Oh, that my ways were directed to keep Your statutes! Then I would not be ashamed, when I look into all Your commandments. I will praise You with uprightness of heart, when I learn Your righteous judgments. I will keep Your statutes; oh, do not forsake me utterly!

Beth

How can a young man cleanse his way? By taking heed according to Your word. With my whole heart I have sought You; oh, let me not wander from Your commandments! Your word I have hidden in my heart, that I might not sin against You. Blessed are You, O Lord! Teach me Your statutes. With my lips I have declared all the judgments of Your mouth. I have rejoiced in the way of Your testimonies, as much as in all riches. I will meditate on Your precepts, and contemplate Your ways. I will delight myself in Your statutes; I will not forget Your word.

Gimel

Deal bountifully with Your servant, that I may live and keep Your word. Open my eyes, that I may see wondrous things from Your law. I am a stranger in the earth; do not hide Your commandments from me. My soul breaks with longing for Your judgments at all times. You rebuke the proud—the cursed, who stray from Your commandments. Remove from me reproach and contempt, for I have kept Your testimonies. Princes also sit and speak against me, but Your servant meditates on Your statutes. Your testimonies also are my delight and my counselors.

Daleth

My soul clings to the dust; revive me according to Your word. I have declared my ways, and You answered me; teach me Your statutes. Make me understand the way of Your precepts; so shall I meditate on Your wonderful works. My soul melts from heaviness; strengthen me according to Your word. Remove from me the way of lying, and grant me Your law graciously. I have chosen the way of truth; Your judgments I have laid before me. I cling to Your testimonies; O Lord, do not

put me to shame! I will run the course of Your com-
mandments, for You shall enlarge my heart.

He

Teach me, O Lord, the way of Your statutes, and I
shall keep it to the end. Give me understanding, and
I shall keep Your law; indeed, I shall observe it with
my whole heart. Make me walk in the path of Your
commandments, for I delight in it. Incline my heart to
Your testimonies, and not to covetousness. Turn away
my eyes from looking at worthless things, and revive
me in Your way. Establish Your word to Your servant,
who is devoted to fearing You. Turn away my reproach
which I dread, for Your judgments are good. Behold, I
long for Your precepts; revive me in Your righteousness.

Waw

Let Your mercies come also to me, O Lord—Your sal-
vation according to Your word. So shall I have an
answer for him who reproaches me, for I trust in Your
word. And take not the word of truth utterly out of
my mouth, for I have hoped in Your ordinances. So
shall I keep Your law continually, forever and ever.
And I will walk at liberty, for I seek Your precepts. I
will speak of Your testimonies also before kings, and
will not be ashamed. And I will delight myself in Your
commandments, which I love. My hands also I will lift
up to Your commandments, which I love, and I will
meditate on Your statutes.

Zayin

Remember the word to Your servant, upon which You have caused me to hope. This is my comfort in my affliction, for Your word has given me life. The proud have me in great derision, yet I do not turn aside from Your law. I remembered Your judgments of old, O Lord, and have comforted myself. Indignation has taken hold of me because of the wicked, who forsake Your law. Your statutes have been my songs in the house of my pilgrimage. I remember Your name in the night, O Lord, and I keep Your law. This has become mine, because I kept Your precepts.

Heth

You are my portion, O Lord; I have said that I would keep Your words. I entreated Your favor with my whole heart; be merciful to me according to Your word. I thought about my ways, and turned my feet to Your testimonies. I made haste, and did not delay to keep Your commandments. The cords of the wicked have bound me, but I have not forgotten Your law. At midnight I will rise to give thanks to You, because of Your righteous judgments. I am a companion of all who fear You, and of those who keep Your precepts. The earth, O Lord, is full of Your mercy; teach me Your statutes.

Teth

You have dealt well with Your servant, O Lord, according to Your word. Teach me good judgment

*and knowledge, for I believe Your commandments.
Before I was afflicted I went astray, but now I keep
Your word. You are good, and do good; teach me Your
statutes. The proud have forged a lie against me, but
I will keep Your precepts with my whole heart. Their
heart is as fat as grease, but I delight in Your law. It is
good for me that I have been afflicted, that I may learn
Your statutes. The law of Your mouth is better to me
than thousands of coins of gold and silver.*

Yod

*Your hands have made me and fashioned me; give
me understanding, that I may learn Your commandments. Those who fear You will be glad when they
see me, because I have hoped in Your word. I know,
O Lord, that Your judgments are right, and that in
faithfulness You have afflicted me. Let, I pray, Your
merciful kindness be for my comfort, according to Your
word to Your servant. Let Your tender mercies come
to me, that I may live; for Your law is my delight. Let
the proud be ashamed, for they treated me wrongfully
with falsehood; but I will meditate on Your precepts.
Let those who fear You turn to me, those who know
Your testimonies. Let my heart be blameless regarding
Your statutes, that I may not be ashamed.*

Kaph

*My soul faints for Your salvation, but I hope in Your
word. My eyes fail from searching Your word, saying,
"When will You comfort me?" For I have become like*

a wineskin in smoke, yet I do not forget Your statutes. How many are the days of Your servant? When will You execute judgment on those who persecute me? The proud have dug pits for me, which is not according to Your law. All Your commandments are faithful; they persecute me wrongfully; help me! They almost made an end of me on earth, but I did not forsake Your precepts. Revive me according to Your lovingkindness, so that I may keep the testimony of Your mouth.

Lamed

Forever, O Lord, Your word is settled in heaven. Your faithfulness endures to all generations; You established the earth, and it abides. They continue this day according to Your ordinances, for all are Your servants. Unless Your law had been my delight, I would then have perished in my affliction. I will never forget Your precepts, for by them You have given me life. I am Yours, save me; for I have sought Your precepts. The wicked wait for me to destroy me, but I will consider Your testimonies. I have seen the consummation of all perfection, but Your commandment is exceedingly broad.

Mem

Oh, how I love Your law! It is my meditation all the day. You, through Your commandments, make me wiser than my enemies; for they are ever with me. I have more understanding than all my teachers, for Your testimonies are my meditation. I understand more than the ancients, because I keep Your precepts. I have restrained my feet from every evil way, that I may keep Your word. I have not departed from Your judgments, for You Yourself have taught me. How sweet are Your words to my taste, sweeter than honey to my mouth! Through Your precepts I get understanding; therefore I hate every false way.

Nun

Your word is a lamp to my feet and a light to my path. I have sworn and confirmed that I will keep Your righteous judgments. I am afflicted very much; revive me, O Lord, according to Your word. Accept, I pray, the freewill offerings of my mouth, O Lord, and teach me Your judgments. My life is continually in my hand, yet I do not forget Your law. The wicked have laid a snare for me, yet I have not strayed from Your precepts. Your testimonies I have taken as a heritage forever, for they are the rejoicing of my heart. I have inclined my heart to perform Your statutes forever, to the very end.

Samek

I hate the double-minded, but I love Your law. You are my hiding place and my shield; I hope in Your word. Depart from me, you evildoers, for I will keep the commandments of my God! Uphold me according to Your word, that I may live; and do not let me be ashamed of my hope. Hold me up, and I shall be safe, and I shall observe Your statutes continually. You reject all those who stray from Your statutes, for their deceit is falsehood. You put away all the wicked of the earth like dross; therefore I love Your testimonies. My flesh trembles for fear of You, and I am afraid of Your judgments.

Ayin

I have done justice and righteousness; do not leave me to my oppressors. Be surety for Your servant for good; do not let the proud oppress me. My eyes fail from seeking Your salvation and Your righteous word. Deal with Your servant according to Your mercy, and teach me Your statutes. I am Your servant; give me understanding, that I may know Your testimonies. It is time for You to act, O Lord, for they have regarded Your law as void. Therefore I love Your commandments more than gold, yes, than fine gold! Therefore all Your precepts concerning all things I consider to be right; I hate every false way.

Pe

Your testimonies are wonderful; therefore my soul keeps them. The entrance of Your words gives light; it gives understanding to the simple. I opened my mouth and panted, for I longed for Your commandments. Look upon me and be merciful to me, as Your custom is toward those who love Your name. Direct my steps by Your word, and let no iniquity have dominion over me. Redeem me from the oppression of man, that I may keep Your precepts. Make Your face shine upon Your servant, and teach me Your statutes.

Rivers of water run down from my eyes, because men do not keep Your law.

Tsadde

Righteous are You, O Lord, and upright are Your judgments. Your testimonies, which You have commanded, are righteous and very faithful. My zeal has consumed me, because my enemies have forgotten Your words. Your word is very pure; therefore Your servant loves it. I am small and despised, yet I do not forget Your precepts. Your righteousness is an everlasting righteousness, and Your law is truth. Trouble and anguish have overtaken me, yet Your commandments are my delights. The righteousness of Your testimonies is everlasting; give me understanding, and I shall live.

Qoph

I cry out with my whole heart; hear me, O Lord! I will keep Your statutes. I cry out to You; save me, and I will keep Your testimonies. I rise before the dawning of the morning, and cry for help; I hope in Your word. My eyes are awake through the night watches, that I may meditate on Your word. Hear my voice according to Your lovingkindness; O Lord, revive me according to Your justice. They draw near who follow after wickedness; they are far from Your law. You are near, O Lord, and all Your commandments are truth. Concerning Your testimonies, I have known of old that You have founded them forever.

Resh

Consider my affliction and deliver me, for I do not forget Your law. Plead my cause and redeem me; revive me according to Your word. Salvation is far from the wicked, for they do not seek Your statutes. Great are Your tender mercies, O Lord; revive me according to Your judgments. Many are my persecutors and my enemies, yet I do not turn from Your testimonies. I see the treacherous, and am disgusted, because they do not keep Your word. Consider how I love Your precepts; revive me, O Lord, according to Your lovingkindness. The entirety of Your word is truth, and every one of Your righteous judgments endures forever.

Shin

Princes persecute me without a cause, but my heart stands in awe of Your word. I rejoice at Your word as one who finds great treasure. I hate and abhor lying, but I love Your law. Seven times a day I praise You, because of Your righteous judgments. Great peace have those who love Your law, and nothing causes them to stumble. Lord, I hope for Your salvation, and I do Your commandments. My soul keeps Your testimonies, and I love them exceedingly. I keep Your precepts and Your testimonies, for all my ways are before You.

Tau

Let my cry come before You, O Lord; give me understanding according to Your word. Let my supplication come before You; deliver me according to Your word. My lips shall utter praise, for You teach me Your statutes. My tongue shall speak of Your word, for all Your commandments are righteousness. Let Your hand become my help, for I have chosen Your precepts. I long for Your salvation, O Lord, and Your law is my delight. Let my soul live, and it shall praise You; and let Your judgments help me. I have gone astray like a lost sheep; seek Your servant, for I do not forget Your commandments.

He sent His word and healed them, and delivered them from their destructions (Psalm 107:20).

Chapter 9

THE BATTLE STRATEGIES OF HEAVEN

For though we walk in the flesh, we do not war according to the flesh. For the weapons of our warfare are not carnal but mighty in God for pulling down strongholds, casting down arguments and every high thing that exalts itself against the knowledge of God, bringing every thought into captivity to the obedience of Christ, and being ready to punish all disobedience when your obedience is fulfilled.
—2 CORINTHIANS 10:3-6

There are angel armies, and they are innumerable. These armies are always available to execute the will of the Most High God. Every angel knows exactly what to do to advance the Kingdom of God effectively. The Most High God has written books concerning every human individual who has ever lived and every individual who will ever live. These books contain all of the wonderful plans God has for His creation, humankind.

Man was created in the image of God. No other creation was made in God's own image. When I was with Jesus in 1992, I was amazed to note how intricately our Creator has made mankind. One thing that I learned while with Jesus is this truth: the Father's desire was to create us as He is. God made us in the image of Himself for one purpose—so that we could interact with Him. Another divine revelation that the Lord made clear to me while I was with Jesus was this truth: man was never made to die or to fall into sin. Human beings were not created to operate and function in the environment that entered the earth when Adam fell from grace.

God created man as perfect in the beginning. God intended that mankind would have complete authority over everything on the earth. The command of mankind would have created anything that man ever desired. Just as our Creator is able to produce things quickly and easily, mankind was to also be able to create things quickly and easily. Before the fall, man operated at a much higher level than presently upon this earth, and God enjoyed fellowship with man.

Angels are sent to help us and are assigned to us to minister for us. "Are they not all ministering spirits sent forth to minister for those who will inherit salvation?" (Heb. 1:14). Special assignments have been given to each of the angels. Angels have the purpose of successfully enforcing what is written in each individual's book. The angels do a great deal of planning to ensure that each person is victorious in his or her destiny. Angels are specifically assigned to certain individuals. Angels are responsible to research and to know every individual under their care. Man will rule and reign with Jesus Christ in the next age. Therefore, it is very important that angels take care of every believer. Angels help to bring the words that the Lord has spoken over each believer into fruition.

During the time that I was with Jesus, I saw something amazing. In the eyes of Jesus, I saw the day that He first thought of me and breathed me into my mother's womb as a living soul. There have been books written about me that tell of my destiny. My destiny is sealed with Him. Angels were assigned to me. My angels have battle strategies for my life that are extremely well-planned. The purpose God has given angels is to enforce everything that God has in His heart for every individual. We must dwell in Him and walk with Him humbly before the Lord for our destiny to come forth.

You formed my innermost being, shaping my delicate inside and my intricate outside, and wove them all together in my mother's womb. I thank you, God, for making me so mysteriously complex! Everything you do is marvelously breathtaking. It simply amazes me to think about it! How thoroughly you know me, Lord! You even formed every bone in my body when you created me in the secret place, carefully, skillfully shaping me from nothing to something. You saw who you created me to be before I became me! Before I'd ever seen the light of day, the number of days you planned for me were already recorded in your book. Every single moment you are thinking of me! How precious and wonderful to consider that you cherish me constantly in your every thought! O God, your desires toward

me are more than the grains of sand on every shore!
When I awake each morning, you're still with me
(Psalm 139:13-18 TPT).

On this earth, every Christian lives where principalities, powers, and the unclean spirits seek to destroy every believer's divine destiny. Angels are assigned to fight back every evil work of the enemy. However, believers are also called to engage in the warfare. Believers must engage in spiritual warfare with prayer and confession. Christians are meant to fight the battle to enforce the borders of God's kingdom as those borders move forward. Every individual who comes to the Lord begins training in the specific areas in which he or she can excel. To the Lord, the most important thing concerning any believer is his or her character. Therefore, every Christian must pass certain tests. Each test that a Christian passes brings promotion in the Kingdom. When Christians begin to realize how important our warfare is to this generation upon the earth today, that revelation will motivate each believer. Every believer will be set on fire by the Holy Spirit and be filled with joy. The revelation of the sons of God in this day will become more and more evident to the world as many of God's own pass the tests that God permits. Each believer will enter into the specific role in this end-time scenario that the Lord has assigned to him or her.

This final, mighty move of God in the glory has already begun. The angels have been sent and are positioning individuals everywhere for the end-time harvest. Many will be saved and delivered in meetings that previously have been fully coordinated in the command center of Heaven. The God of angel armies is presently coordinating each believer's breakthrough. God Almighty is sending every Christian the help that he or she needs to ensure that every believer will pass all of these tests in life. Angels are fully equipped to fight any enemy that comes against every single believer. Angels are aware that someday believers will rule over them. They will not only assist every believer now, in this present life, but they will also assist every believer in the life to come. Angels will help each Christian with whatever he or she is specifically assigned to do for the Lord and His Kingdom.

WEAPONS/WARFARE[1]

Weapon (n)

1. Any instrument of offense; anything used or designed to be used in destroying or annoying an enemy.

2. An instrument for contest, or for combating enemies.

The weapons of our warfare are not carnal (2 Corinthians 10:4).

3. An instrument of defense.

Warfare (n)

1. Military service; military life; war.

The Philistines gathered their armies for warfare (1 Samuel 28:1).

2. Contest; struggle with spiritual enemies.

The weapons of our warfare are not carnal (2 Corinthians 10:4).

Warfare (verb intransitive)

To lead a military life; to carry on continual wars.

THE ARMOR OF GOD

Finally, my brethren, be strong in the Lord and in the power of His might. Put on the whole armor of God, that you may be able to stand against the wiles of the devil. For we do not wrestle against flesh and blood, but against principalities, against powers, against the rulers of the darkness of this age, against spiritual hosts of wickedness in the heavenly places. Therefore take up the whole armor of God, that you may be able to withstand in the evil day, and having done all, to stand. Stand therefore, having girded your waist with truth, having put on the breastplate of righteousness, and having shod your feet with the preparation of the gospel of peace; above all, taking the shield of faith with which you will be able to quench all the fiery darts of the wicked one. And take the helmet of salvation, and the sword of the Spirit, which is the word of God; praying always with all prayer and supplication in the Spirit, being watchful to this end with all perseverance and supplication for all the saints— and for me, that utterance may be given to me, that I may open my mouth boldly to make known the mystery of the gospel, for which I am an ambassador in chains; that in it I may speak boldly, as I ought to speak (Ephesians 6:10-20).

In Ephesians 6, there are some crucial verses that every Christian must understand. This important information has to do with *the battle strategies of Heaven*. Every Christian's assignment on this earth is exceedingly powerful and includes working with angels. Every Christian must have an understanding of *the battle strategies of Heaven* to fulfill his or her destiny upon the earth.

There are four very important briefings that Christians need to understand to assist God. Christians have a part in helping God on the earth today. Ephesians 6 highlights the following principles:

1. **Briefing one: Be strong in the Lord and in the power of His might.**

2. **Briefing two: Put on the whole armor of God.**
   - That you may be able to stand against the wiles of the devil.

3. **Briefing three: *For we do not wrestle against flesh and blood,* but against all of these elements:**
   - Principalities.
   - Powers.
   - The rulers of the darkness of this age.
   - Spiritual hosts of wickedness in the heavenly places.

4. **Briefing four: Therefore take up the whole armor of God.**
   - That you may be able to withstand in the evil day.
   - Having done all, to stand.
   - Stand therefore.
   - Having girded your waist with truth.
   - Having put on the breastplate of righteousness.

- Having shod your feet with the preparation of the gospel of peace.

- Taking the shield of faith.

- You will be able to quench all the fiery darts of the wicked one.

- Take the helmet of salvation.

- Take the sword of the Spirit.

  - Which is the word of God.

- Praying always with all prayer and supplication.

  - In the Spirit.

- Being watchful to this end with:

  - All perseverance.

  - All supplication.

  - For all the saints.

  - For me, that utterance may be given to me.

  - That I may open my mouth boldly to make known the mystery of the gospel.

  - For which I am an ambassador in chains.

  - That in it I may speak boldly.

  - As I ought to speak.

In briefing one, *be strong in the Lord and in the power of His might*, every believer must understand and grasp the concepts of warfare. One of the most important concepts of warfare is this one: Christians must realize that no believer will ever lose if he or she will stay in the strength of the Lord. He is our Commander, leader of the angel armies. Christians will be well able to face any opponent, knowing that we will always win every battle. Christians have all of God's power and assistance readily available. There are myriads of angels available to fight with every Christian, so there is no need to fear what may come. Christians are to be strong in every battle because the Lord God our Commander is ever with His own in battle.

In briefing two, *put on the whole armor of God,* believers must be fully dressed for war. Believers must rest assured that no weapon formed against them will ever prosper because Christians are clothed in the proper battle equipment but are also well-trained to use the weapons of our warfare. Every believer will stand against the battle strategies of the devil. He is already a defeated enemy. Every believer must step forward and take a stand against the enemy of our souls. Every Christian has the right to watch the enemy flee in terror because every believer will submit to our Commander. God is all-powerful and has given every believer divine authority in His Kingdom to defeat the enemy.

In briefing three, *for we do not wrestle against flesh and blood,* Christians learn the different classifications and ranks of our enemy. As believers join forces against these four levels of the enemy, they have complete confidence in their God-given authority over these forces. Additionally, the angels are always with the believers to assist them. Christians will drive the enemy back to the borders of the Kingdom. Christians are free to use the precious blood of Jesus and the name of Jesus against these defeated enemies. Every believer will come against the principalities, powers, rulers of the darkness of this age, and spiritual hosts of wickedness in the heavenly places. Believers will render these enemies of our soul powerless against God's army.

In briefing four, *therefore take up the whole armor of God,* Christians begin to rise up and come against evil. Believers will stand firm in all the authority and dominion of God Almighty. Each Christian's waist is wrapped in truth. Each Christian's chest is protected with the breastplate of righteousness. Each Christian's feet are prepared with the gospel of peace. Believers take the good news everywhere they go. The blessing of God operates in every Christian's life because of the peace of God, His shalom. Christians use the shield of faith that quenches all the fiery darts of the wicked one. Every believer's head is protected by the helmet of salvation. All Christians will use the sword of the spirit, which is the Word of God, to cut down the enemy with the truth. Every believer will use the sword of the spirit as a very effective weapon against those evil spirits who attempt to stop the answer to every prayer. Christians will pray continually with all kinds of prayer and supplication. As a good soldier in Christ, each believer will pray in the Spirit always, building up the most holy faith and remaining in the love of God. Christians will be watchful to the very end in all perseverance for all the saints, praying for everyone to have boldness to speak and make known the mystery of the gospel.

> *The Lord will cause your enemies who rise against you to be defeated before your face. They shall come out against you one way and flee before you seven ways* (Deuteronomy 28:7).

SECRET BATTLE STRATEGY CHECKLIST

Submission to Authority

Therefore submit to God. Resist the devil and he will flee from you (James 4:7).

The Greater One

You are of God, little children, and have overcome them, because He who is in you is greater than he who is in the world (1 John 4:4).

Divine Power

For though we live in the world, we do not wage war as the world does. The weapons we fight with are not the weapons of the world. On the contrary, they have divine power to demolish strongholds. We demolish arguments and every pretension that sets itself up against the knowledge of God, and we take captive every thought to make it obedient to Christ (2 Corinthians 10:3-5 NIV).

Stand Firm in Faith

Be sober, be vigilant; because your adversary the devil walks about like a roaring lion, seeking whom he may devour. Resist him, steadfast in the faith (1 Peter 5:8-9).

No Weapon Will Prosper

"No weapon formed against you shall prosper, and every tongue which rises against you in judgment you

shall condemn. This is the heritage of the servants of the Lord, and their righteousness is from Me," says the Lord (Isaiah 54:17).

Full Armor

Put on the full armor of God, so that you can take your stand against the devil's schemes. For our struggle is not against flesh and blood, but against the rulers, against the authorities, against the powers of this dark world and against the spiritual forces of evil in the heavenly realms. Therefore put on the full armor of God, so that when the day of evil comes, you may be able to stand your ground, and after you have done everything, to stand. Stand firm then, with the belt of truth buckled around your waist, with the breastplate of righteousness in place, and with your feet fitted with the readiness that comes from the gospel of peace. In addition to all this, take up the shield of faith, with which you can extinguish all the flaming arrows of the evil one. Take the helmet of salvation and the sword of the Spirit, which is the word of God (Ephesians 6:11-17 NIV).

More than Conquerors

In all these things we are more than conquerors through Him who loved us (Romans. 8:37).

Victory

But thanks be to God, who gives us the victory through our Lord Jesus Christ (1 Corinthians 15:57).

By My Spirit

"Not by might nor by power, but by My Spirit," says the Lord of hosts (Zechariah 4:6).

Protection

But the Lord is faithful, and he will strengthen you and protect you from the evil one (2 Thessalonians 3:3 NIV).

Authority

Behold, I have given you authority to tread on serpents and scorpions, and over all the power of the enemy, and nothing shall hurt you (Luke 10:19 ESV).

Abundant Life

The thief comes only to steal and kill and destroy. I came that they may have life and have it abundantly (John 10:10 ESV).

Agreement

Truly I tell you, whatever you bind on earth will be bound in heaven, and whatever you loose on earth will be loosed in heaven. Again, truly I tell you that if two of you on earth agree about anything they ask for, it will be done for them by my Father in heaven (Matthew 18:18-19 NIV).

Enemies Defeated

The Lord will cause your enemies who rise against you to be defeated before your face. They shall come out against you one way and flee before you seven ways (Deuteronomy 28:7).

Overcome

I have told you these things, so that in me you may have peace. In this world you will have trouble. But take heart! I have overcome the world (John 16:33 NIV).

A Way Out

No temptation has overtaken you except what is common to mankind. And God is faithful; he will not let you be tempted beyond what you can bear. But when you are tempted, he will also provide a way out so that you can endure it (1 Corinthians 10:13 NIV).

Truth

And you will know the truth, and the truth will set you free (John 8:32 NLT).

Overcome Evil

Do not be overcome by evil, but overcome evil with good (Romans 12:21).

Blood of the Lamb

And they have conquered him by the blood of the Lamb and by the word of their testimony, for they loved not their lives even unto death (Revelation 12:11 ESV).

The Good Fight

Fight the good fight of the faith. Take hold of the eternal life to which you were called when you made your good confession in the presence of many witnesses (1 Timothy 6:12 NIV).

The Rock

On this rock I will build My church, and the gates of Hades shall not prevail against it (Matthew 16:18).

Victorious Son of God

The reason the Son of God appeared was to destroy the devil's work (1 John 3:8 NIV).

Wait on the Lord

But they who wait for the Lord shall renew their strength; they shall mount up with wings like eagles; they shall run and not be weary; they shall walk and not faint (Isaiah 40:31 ESV).

The Lord Who Fights for You

One of your men puts to flight a thousand, for the Lord your God is He who fights for you, just as He promised you (Joshua 23:10 NASB).

The God Who Fights for You

Do not fear them, for the Lord your God is the one fighting for you (Deuteronomy 3:22 NASB).

God Is for Us

What then shall we say to these things? If God is for us, who can be against us? (Romans 8:31)

The God Who Pushes Back

Through You we will push back our adversaries; through Your name we will trample down those who rise up against us (Psalm 44:5 NASB).

Strong and Courageous

Have I not commanded you? Be strong and courageous! Do not tremble or be dismayed, for the Lord your God is with you wherever you go (Joshua 1:9 NASB).

Overthrow

For You have girded me with strength for battle; You have subdued under me those who rose up against me (Psalm 18:39 NASB).

My Refuge

He who dwells in the shelter of the Most High will abide in the shadow of the Almighty. I will say to the Lord, "My refuge and my fortress, my God, in whom I trust!" For it is He who delivers you from the snare of the trapper and from the deadly pestilence. He will cover you with His pinions, and under His wings you may seek refuge; His faithfulness is a shield and bulwark (Psalm 91:1-4 NASB).

The Battle Is Yours

> *This is what the Lord says to you: "Do not be afraid or discouraged because of this vast army. For the battle is not yours, but God's"* (2 Chronicles 20:15 NIV).

NOTE

1. *Noah Webster's Dictionary of the English Language,* 1828 edition. Public domain.

Chapter 10

THE WILL OF GOD FOR EVERY CHRISTIAN'S LIFE

*And do not be conformed to this world, but be transformed
by the renewing of your mind, that you may prove what
is that good and acceptable and perfect will of God .*
—ROMANS 12:2

Right now, believers will experience an amazing time in the Kingdom of God. As the world enters the mighty move of God that will fill the earth with His glory, every Christian must also know the specific will of God for his or her life. God's perfect will and His perfect destiny will begin to come forth in the lives of Christians. God is preparing to return to the earth soon. God's agenda is to dramatically influence the life of every believer. His touch on the lives of every Christian comes through the angels. Angels minister to believers. Their purpose is to expedite life in the Spirit so that every Christian is able to walk in the narrow way, which is not always an easy way. However, along that narrow way, God helps believers to learn important principles that will enable each Christian to fulfill his or her destiny. The Lord helps each person learn those things that he or she must learn so that his or her life can be successful. God guides every believer who will walk that narrow way to experience things that will cause him or her to be very powerful victors for His Kingdom. A believer's transformation into a powerful Christian warrior has a crucial element that every believer must possess. That element is complete trust in the Lord.

TRUST HIM

God is a person of His Word, and therefore Christians can fully trust in Him. When the Lord says what will happen, it is absolutely going to happen. The will of God for a Christian's life is based on an eternal purpose that God Almighty has for each person. God planned His perfect will for each believer before the world was formed. God actually thought about every person who would ever come to the knowledge of Christ. Jesus Christ was the Lamb who was slain before the foundations of the world. God had it in His heart to create a plan for every Christian. And He had that plan ready before the earth was even formed. The Lord makes it possible for every Christian, in this life, to know His perfect will. No one needs to be in the dark about God's will for his or her life. The angels will always be present to assist every believer in any way to move into the center of what our Almighty God is doing. In this last and greatest move of God that the earth has already begun to experience, angels are especially prepared to help every Christian triumph in every battle that he or she may face. Christians need to recognize this spiritual truth—the spirit is willing, but the flesh is weak.

In the Spirit realm, angels desire to implement the perfect will of God into every believer's life. Yet believers often do not know what God's specific will may be for a situation. Our lack of knowledge is possibly due to the fact that Christians do not understand what the Lord is revealing at a given moment in time. Christians sometimes are trying to figure out if they are in the perfect will of God or if they are in the permissive will God. Being unable to comprehend God's will for one's life has a solution. The counsel of the Holy Spirit will provide an answer for this situation. The Holy Spirit can always instruct a Christian in the way that he or she should go.

The Spirit of God comes to every believer as the sword of the Spirit. The sword of the Spirit will divide between the soul and the spirit.

> *For the word of God is living and powerful, and sharper than any two-edged sword, piercing even to the division of soul and spirit, and of joints and marrow, and is a discerner of the thoughts and intents of the heart* (Hebrews 4:12).

THE SWORD OF THE SPIRIT

The Spirit of God created each person's soul with three components—the mind, the will, and the emotions. The real person in each individual is found within someone's soul. When the Spirit of truth comes, He reveals absolute truth and leads every believer into his or her destiny. The Spirit of truth lives inside of every believer. Because the Spirit of truth dwells within each Christian, each believer has revelation occurring within him or within her at all times. That revelation comes to each Christian in his or her spirit. Every Christian must allow the revelation to have access to his or her mind. A believer's body does not naturally desire to do the will of God. As human beings, Christians often want to ask questions and reason out the things of the Spirit. Christians often face an interior battle between the spirit and the mind and the flesh. The mind wants to do things its own way. The flesh wants to do things its own way as well. Christians must be governed by the leading of the Holy Spirit.

While this war is going on for preeminence of the spirit or the mind or the flesh, the power of the Holy Spirit lights up the spirit that is inside of every individual. The born-again experience actually is the Spirit entering into the person's spirit. The spirit that exists within a person is actually the light of God that dwells inside of every Christian. The angels of the Lord do an amazing work—they help draw people to Christ, causing them to be in a place where they are ready to accept the Lord Jesus as Savior. Angels, working behind the scenes, prepare a spiritual atmosphere that causes people to recognize their personal need for the Lord. At the very moment that any person becomes a Christian, he or she enters a position of acceptance of the things of God. This is an amazing change in a person's life. One who was once reluctant to give himself or herself over to the Lord completely reverses his or her stance to become a person who will accept God completely.

According to God's Word, every born-again person becomes a new creation. Second Corinthians 5:17 says, "Therefore, if anyone is in Christ, he is a new creation; old things have passed away; behold, all things have become new." A Christian's spirit is full of the resurrection power of God. However, every soul must also be renewed. This renewal or transformation happens when the Word of God changes a person's mindset.

> *And do not be conformed to this world, but be transformed by the renewing of your mind, that you may prove what is that good and acceptable and perfect will of God* (Romans 12:2).

THE LORD LIGHTS ME UP

The apostle Paul said that every believer must discipline his or her body. Each person must make the physical body comply with the inner man's desires. The spirit man is the heart of man. A person's spirit is supposed to be the master of his or her life. A person's spirit is perfect because it has been transformed by the Spirit of God. One's spirit is the place where God dwells. A person is not complete in his or her soul or body. One must allow the Lord to renew and transform his or her soul. As a Christian opens himself or herself to divine revelation, his or her soul becomes alight with the Spirit of God. Second Samuel 22:29-37 says:

> *For You are my lamp, O Lord; the Lord shall enlighten my darkness. For by You I can run against a troop; by*

my God I can leap over a wall. As for God, His way is perfect; the word of the Lord is proven; He is a shield to all who trust in Him. For who is God, except the Lord? And who is a rock, except our God? God is my strength and power, and He makes my way perfect. He makes my feet like the feet of deer, and sets me on my high places. He teaches my hands to make war, so that my arms can bend a bow of bronze. You have also given me the shield of Your salvation; Your gentleness has made me great. You enlarged my path under me; so my feet did not slip.

Second Samuel 22 contains much wisdom of the Lord. The Lord God is delighted to live inside of you. Proverbs 20:27 says, "The spirit of a man is the lamp of the Lord, searching all the inner depths of his heart." The Spirit lights the spirit of man. The Spirit also lights each believer's path. As the light of God enters into one's spirit, that light will work its way out into a person's soul and also to his or her understanding. Revelation arises in a believer in a similar way to what the apostle Paul mentioned concerning praying in the spirit. He said in First Corinthians 14:2, "For one who speaks in an unknown tongue does not speak to people but to God; for no one understands him or catches his meaning, but by the Spirit he speaks mysteries [secret truths, hidden things]" (AMP).

PRAYING PERFECT PRAYERS

It is important to realize what Paul is saying about divine mysteries being spoken into our realm of understanding. When someone prays in tongues and interprets that prayer, he or she is actually praying out the perfect will of God for his or her life. That prayer is done by the Spirit, and one's mind does not actually participate in bringing the revelation forth. The Spirit of God moves in our weakness. The Holy Spirit is a Helper. He takes hold of every believer in his or her weakness and prays out the mysteries through each person. The Holy Spirit prays these mysteries out according to the will of God. The best situation for every Christian is to be in the perfect will of God for his or her life. The apostle Paul says:

> *And in a similar way, the Holy Spirit takes hold of us in our human frailty to empower us in our weakness. For example, at times we don't even know how to pray, or know the best things to ask for. But the Holy Spirit rises up within us to super-intercede on our behalf, pleading to God with emotional sighs too deep for words. God, the searcher of the heart, knows fully our longings, yet he also understands the desires of the Spirit, because the Holy Spirit passionately pleads before God for us, his holy ones, in perfect harmony with God's plan and our destiny. So we are convinced that every detail of our lives is continually woven together to fit into God's perfect plan of bringing good into our lives, for we are his lovers who have been called to fulfill his designed purpose. For he knew all about us before we were born and he destined us from the beginning to share the likeness of his Son. This means the Son is the oldest among a vast family of brothers and sisters who will become just like him. Having determined our destiny ahead of time, he called us to himself and transferred his perfect righteousness to everyone he called. And*

*those who possess his perfect righteousness he co-glori-
fied with his Son!* (Romans 8:26-30 TPT)

The Holy Spirit is sent as the *Standby* to be there always for
every believer. The Holy Spirit wants to pray out the mysteries of
God in every Christian's spirit. However, sometimes a person's
mind does not comprehend what the Holy Spirit is speaking. A
person can ask God to help him or her to understand what the
Spirit is saying. If one is able to receive the interpretation of what
the Spirit is saying, and he or she receives full understanding, that
is wonderful. However, many Christians do not reach that level
of interpretation. With persistence and continued experience in
praying in tongues, it is more and more likely that a Christian will
begin to interpret the tongues that he or she speaks in individual
prayer. When a Christian prays in tongues, he or she is actually
praying out the mysteries of God. The Lord helps a Spirit-filled
Christian to pray out the perfect will of God in tongues. The
Lord told King David that the Spirit of the Lord would bring him
to the perfect path. "You will show me the path of life; in Your
presence is fullness of joy; at Your right hand are pleasures forever-
more" (Ps. 16:11).

Every Christian can be on the particular path of life that
God has chosen for him or her. The angels are walking with every
believer along this path. Angels help usher Christians into His
presence. They help Christians be full of joy. One of the things
that every Christian must assess is the joy level that he or she possesses. Joy must come! Joy is part of the perfect will of God for
every believer. There are definitely times when a Christian actually is in the perfect will of God, even though some difficult things
happen. One's life will not always be smooth. However every
believer has access to peace and joy. Each believer must recognize

that God is with him or her and that He takes care of everything. For example, although the apostle Paul was shipwrecked, he knew that he was going to survive because an angel had appeared to him with good news. Paul's angels appeared to him at different times, revealing that everything would work out successfully. They told Paul what was going to happen, and it happened exactly as the angels had told him. The angels were sent to minister to Paul and encourage him. In the Book of Psalms David says, "Teach me Your way, O Lord, and lead me in a smooth path, because of my enemies" (Ps. 27:11).

TEACH ME

It should be the desire of every Christian to have God to teach them His way and lead them on a smooth path. Every single Christian needs the Lord's instruction and guidance to defeat the enemies of the faith. Angels are sent to protect God's own from our enemies. Angels also guide each believer on the path that God has for each Christian. God mentions leading His children upon a smooth path; therefore, believers can be certain that a smooth path is possible. The Holy Spirit knows the deep secrets of God. Within the heart of man, the Holy Spirit is an instructor. The Spirit reveals these deep mysteries to every Christian through the Christian's spirit. The Holy Spirit lights every believer's path, providing understanding for him or her. As believers heed His direction, the Holy Spirit will help conform each Christian to the Word of God. Psalm 139 says:

> *O Lord, You have searched me and known me. You know my sitting down and my rising up; You under-stand my thought afar off. You comprehend my path*

*and my lying down, and are acquainted with all my
ways* (Psalm 139:1-3).

God is acquainted with all our ways. Angels are acquainted
with God's ways. Christians must begin to understand the agenda
of angels. Angels have been sent to implement the will of God in
each believer's life. Angels exist for one purpose—to help every
Christian know the will of God. In the spirit realm, many angels
exist. The angels' purpose is to do the will of God. Everybody
in Heaven is excited. They clearly comprehend the plan of God
for this generation. Angels are certain that the victory will come
for every Christian through Jesus Christ. Angels are sent to help
believers after they have read the book for every believer. Each
angel understands God's plan for the believers they are to assist.
They know the strategies that will bring victory for this generation. Angels target evil spirits to drive them out and uproot
them from evil influence in the lives of Christians. Angels arrive
to help each Christian, so every believer must submit his or her
will to God's will. The path to victory for every Christian is that
Christian's full submission to God's will. God's will is His Word.
His intentions for every believer are great. The prophet Jeremiah
prophesied that God has plans for each person to prosper and for
each person to succeed. You will have a good, expected end (see
Jer. 29:11).

> *Do not remember the former things, nor consider
> the things of old. Behold, I will do a new thing, now
> it shall spring forth; shall you not know it?* (Isaiah
> 43:18-19)

As a person reads this message, he or she is being stirred
within his or her being. The Spirit of God's desire is to bring out

the treasuries of God's wisdom and knowledge concerning each believer. God wants all Christians to know His plan and purpose for them. He wants to make His plan and purpose for every Christian clear. Believers must go through a process, but that process is not always easy. Christians need to realize that not only does God exist in eternity, but He also has already established eternal truth that is absolute.

Christians must recognize that walking in the Spirit requires certain things. Believers must receive spiritual truth in the spirit realm. Believers need to learn to expect the manifestation of that truth into the realm of the earth. The Spirit is unfolding the mysteries of the will of God to believers. The Spirit is revealing the divine plan for this generation. Christians need to stand and boldly speak to this generation. They are to call people back to their first love. The Father God desires that every Christian receive the agenda of angels. The entire generation of believers of today is to come back into alignment with God's heart. After Christians begin working completely to fulfill God's purposes, then the greatest move of the Spirit that has ever touched this earth is going spread as a holy, all-consuming fire.

> *You have also given me the shield of Your salvation; Your right hand has held me up, Your gentleness has made me great. You enlarged my path under me, so my feet did not slip* (Psalm 18:35-36).

Chapter 11

HEAVEN ON EARTH

*In this manner, therefore, pray: Our Father in
heaven, hallowed be Your name. Your kingdom come.
Your will be done on earth as it is in heaven.*
—MATTHEW 6:9-10

Angels are working in every Christian's life. For some believers,
angels may be such a surprise because those believers really did not
actually realize that angels not only do exist, but also have a big

part to do in the work of the Lord. Christians must begin to open themselves to the Spirt of the Lord and the Word of the Lord. God desires that every Christian have a renewed mind, so each believer must open his or her thought life to the new mental perspective that the Holy Spirit will work in each person who will submit to God's renewal process. Each Christian's thoughts must be renewed so he or she will see things from a divine perspective. The renewing of the mind is important because it is essential for victory to be continual in a believer's life. In Romans 12:2, the apostle Paul talks about being transformed by the renewing of your mind through the Word of God. What God speaks is the absolute truth of Heaven. What God speaks is His established will. People wrote the Bible through the act of God breathing upon their lives and through the moving of the Holy Ghost. The inspired Word of God is readily available. We can meditate upon His Word both day and night. Searching the Scriptures will eliminate many questions that a Christian may have concerning the things of the Lord, as well as concerning the things of this life. Every Christian has the obligation to establish his or her life completely upon the will of God in his or her life. God gives His own the truth, as revealed in the Word of God. His Word is the firm foundation for building a Christian life that triumphs in every situation.

Before any Christian was ever born, he or she had a place in the heart of God. Every believer originated in the heart of the Father. He breathed each believer into his or her mother's womb. Several of Jesus's profound statements are explained in this chapter. Jesus said:

> *Pray like this: "Our Father, dwelling in the heavenly realms, may the glory of your name be the center on which our lives turn. Manifest your kingdom realm,*

and cause your every purpose to be fulfilled on earth,
just as it is fulfilled in heaven" (Matthew 6:9-10
TPT).

PRAYING FROM THE
HEAVENLY KINGDOM

When a Christian prays to our Father in Heaven, we mentally
acknowledge that Heaven is already established in the *absolute
truth* of His Kingdom. So when believers pray correctly, they are
acknowledging that His Kingdom is being established in this
physical realm as it is in the heavenly realm as His ambassadors,
Christians, enforce the will of the King on this earth. Christians
speak the word of the King. All authority of His dominion has been
given to God's own.

> *Whoever speaks [to the congregation], is to do so as
> one who speaks the oracles (utterances, the very words)
> of God. Whoever serves [the congregation] is to do so
> as one who serves by the strength which God [abun-
> dantly] supplies, so that in all things God may be glori-
> fied [honored and magnified] through Jesus Christ,
> to whom belongs the glory and dominion forever and
> ever. Amen* (1 Peter 4:11 AMP).

Christians acknowledge satan as the god of this world. He has a
kingdom that will steal, kill, and destroy. Jesus came to give believers life and to give them life more abundantly (see John 10:10). The
Kingdom of God is far beyond what anyone can imagine. When
Jesus came, He spoke with authority. His authority originated from
a realm other than this earth. He spoke from the heavenly realms,

where His Father's Kingdom is established. He came from the place of absolute authority and from the place of absolute truth. He came from the Father. Jesus spoke only those things which His Father spoke to Him. Jesus did not speak on His own. He spoke only what the Father told Him to say.

Jesus announced the Holy Spirit was coming. He said that the Holy Spirit was another one like Him. Jesus referred to the Holy Spirit as the Comforter, Advocate, and Standby. The Holy Spirit will speak only what the Father is saying. The Holy Spirit does the will of God. His desire is to implement the complete will of God in a Christian's life. The will of God, according to Jesus, is to pray Heaven on to the earth. When Christians learn to pray correctly, the influence of Heaven will overtake the spirit of this world. Christians must realize their part to assist in overtaking the kingdoms of this world. The kingdoms of this world must be overtaken by the Kingdom of our God.

Jesus spoke with authority. "And so it was, when Jesus had ended these sayings, that the people were astonished at His teaching, for He taught them as one having authority, and not as the scribes" (Matt. 7:28-29). Jesus spoke from the heavenly Kingdom. His authority originated in the heavenly Kingdom because that is where He existed before He came to the earth.

On the Day of Pentecost, the Holy Spirit, who is inside of every Christian, poured out from the believers. He came with great power and demonstration. The Spirit of God renews every believer's spirit. He dwells within each believer and speaks the truth from Heaven to our spirit. Jesus said that believers can speak to this mountain, and if they believe in their heart that what they say with their mouths, they will have it (see Mark 11:23-24).

Nothing can stop any believer. Jesus said that if a Christian will believe, nothing shall be impossible to him or her (see Mark 9:23).

REMOVE THE LIMITS

Jesus wants every Christian to take belief to a higher level. "Therefore I say to you, whatever things you ask when you pray, believe that you receive them, and you will have them" (Mark 11:24). Jesus said that if a Christian will believe, nothing shall be impossible to them. Christ has removed any limit for a Christian. Christians must realize that victory belongs to them because God places no limits upon what they may ask. Christians must not limit their victories by placing limits upon what the Lord will do in answer to believing. We can observe a person who did take off all of the limits, believing God in faith. Matthew 8 reveals the story of the centurion who believed that Jesus had unlimited power. It is time for Christians to refuse to limit our mighty God.

> *Now when Jesus had entered Capernaum, a centurion came to Him, pleading with Him, saying, "Lord, my servant is lying at home paralyzed, dreadfully tormented." And Jesus said to him, "I will come and heal him." The centurion answered and said, "Lord, I am not worthy that You should come under my roof. But only speak a word, and my servant will be healed. For I also am a man under authority, having soldiers under me. And I say to this one, 'Go,' and he goes; and to another, 'Come,' and he comes; and to my servant, 'Do this,' and he does it." When Jesus heard it, He marveled, and said to those who followed, "Assuredly, I say to you, I have not found such great faith, not even*

in Israel! And I say to you that many will come from east and west, and sit down with Abraham, Isaac, and Jacob in the kingdom of heaven. But the sons of the kingdom will be cast out into outer darkness. There will be weeping and gnashing of teeth." Then Jesus said to the centurion, "Go your way; and as you have believed, so let it be done for you." And his servant was healed that same hour (Matthew 8:5-13).

When Jesus received this request, He did not even consider if answering the request was the perfect will of God. The answer had already been established. Jesus immediately said what He was going to do. Jesus had already established the will of God for this situation. This story is a perfect example of the way Christians should deal with every situation. Believers know that the will of God in Heaven includes no sickness. Therefore, Christians must note that there was no sickness that was the will of God when Jesus went about healing the sick. Jesus did not go around making people sick. The Book of Acts says that Jesus went around doing good, healing everyone who was oppressed the devil (see Acts 10:38). Jesus was continually acting out what the Father was doing in Heaven.

IMPLEMENTATION

Christians must learn how to take what is in Heaven and implement it upon the earth. And believers need to learn how to do this without hesitation. The Spirit desires for every Christian to act as God would have him or her to act, without even thinking about it. Christians must no longer hesitate to do the will of God, and they must know the will of God precisely. Christians must come to the point where they only speak a word, and the will of God is done. Christians must understand their authority and begin to walk in that authority.

Christians need to walk in the power of the *implementation* of the Kingdom without hesitation in these last days. God Almighty and angels have this agenda. Christians desire to see the supernatural power of Heaven in manifestation in the earth. Jesus is taking every believer to a higher level of trust. Christians are beginning to move in the words and actions that cause the supernatural power of God to manifest. Believers are walking in a higher calling today as they become more assured that what they say will come to pass.

A Servant's Heart

But Jesus answered and said, "You do not know what you ask. Are you able to drink the cup that I am about to drink, and be baptized with the baptism that I am baptized with? "They said to Him, "We are able." So He said to them, "You will indeed drink My cup, and be baptized with the baptism that I am baptized with; but to sit on My right hand and on My left is not Mine to give, but it is for those for whom it is prepared by My Father." And when the ten heard it, they were greatly displeased with the two brothers. But Jesus called them to Himself and said, "You know that the rulers of the Gentiles lord it over them, and those who are great exercise authority over them. Yet it shall not be so among you; but whoever desires to become great among you, let him be your servant. And whoever desires to be first among you, let him be your slave—just as the Son of Man did not come to be served, but to serve, and to give His life a ransom for many" (Matthew 20:22-28).

Servanthood is one key to the supernatural power of God. Allowing the heavenly realm to manifest in this life requires that a person understand the effectiveness of serving. Being a servant and taking the lower position allows someone to experience promotion from the Lord. No Christian need push himself or herself forward. When I was with Jesus, I saw that everything I did for someone counted on my record in Heaven. Christians need to be satisfied with serving people. Some Christians need to realize the fact that it is fine to be counted as not the first, but the last. God can use a person, and He will promote the one who is willing to serve. One key to the supernatural realm that the angels understand is that a person must not attempt to push himself or herself forward. The angels are often more intelligent about the things of God than Christians. Angels have the advantage of having seen the books that tell of each Christian's future. Angels have studied in the libraries of Heaven. They see God your Father on the throne and the events in Heaven, yet they come and they serve Christians. Despite the fact that believers do not see angels, the angels still do minister for Christians.

Christians may say that they believe in angels, but if they ever encounter one their view of angels will be transformed. When a Christian has an angel appear, he or she will perhaps be surprised that angels do, indeed, exist. These angels come to serve Christians. Angels do not want the worship of Christians. Angels are not concerned about receiving credit for the things that they do. They want God the Father and God the Son to get the credit for everything. Angels are humble servants of God who do what God says. Jesus announced that He had a secret for all who want to be great in the Kingdom—they must be the least. Christians have absolutely nothing to lose if they give everything up for Him. Christians have been given the power to become children of God.

> *He was in the world, and the world was made through Him, and the world did not know Him.* **He came to His own, and His own did not receive Him.** *But as many as received Him, to them He gave the right to become* **children of God,** *to those who believe in His name: who were born, not of blood, nor of the will of the flesh, nor of the will of man, but of God* (John 1:10-13).

ABIDE IN ME

Believers are born of the Spirit and encounter the will of God. Every Christian has the Spirit of God within himself or herself, and within that innermost being of every Christian is the desire to perform God's will upon earth. The days of Heaven on earth are coming in the power of the Holy Spirit as Christians abide in the vine. Jesus invites believers to see the light of His countenance and encounter His life source when they connect to the vine as branches. A Christian connects to the life flow of the Spirit of God, and that divine flow begins at the throne of God. When a believer taps into that divine flow, then he or she can ask whatever he or she desires. As a believer waits upon Him for the answer, the Lord will move. Christians can have great confidence that God does hear them. The confidence we have comes from the fact that Christians are connected to the vine. Christians can have confidence that God hears them, and in that confidence they can know that He answers.

The life flow is a river of living water that connects every Christian to God. Believers must allow that river to flow through them. Christians will see the manifestation of the full flow of the Spirit of God in the earth. It is time to see Heaven on earth!

> *On the last day, that great day of the feast, Jesus stood and cried out, saying, "If anyone thirsts, let him come to Me and drink. He who believes in Me, as the Scripture has said, out of his heart will flow rivers of living water." But this He spoke concerning the Spirit, whom those believing in Him would receive; for the Holy Spirit was not yet given, because Jesus was not yet glorified* (John 7:37-39).

RIVER OF LIFE

Christians have rivers of living water flowing from them and are actually connected with the throne room of Heaven. The river of life originated at the throne of God. I saw that river when I was in Heaven. It was crystal clear and was like liquid diamonds. It was so beautiful that I just wanted to gaze at it, even though it was so glistening and bright. Then, I wanted to run down and drink from it. I knew that if I would drink from that river, I would live forever. There was no way that I would ever die if I drank that water. The water flows down from the throne room. The river flows into every Christian's spirit and out of every Christian's mouth. When a believer speaks, he or she speaks words that are life and that are spirit. And by speaking life and spirit, each Christian is bringing days of Heaven to the earth.

As a believer, a person can experience the manifestation of the Son of God's ministry in his or her life. Jesus said the works

He did believers will see because His ministry continues through His own. Christians are going to do even greater works because we represent God in the earth. Believers have authority in His name. Believers are able to speak the Word. By speaking the Word, they are able to accomplish God's will in the earth. The river that is flowing out of each Christian helps him or her to ask the correct things of the Lord. That is why when a Christian does ask, her or she will receive. This is the will of God for every believer's life—*answered prayer.* Chapter 15 of the Book of John discusses prayer. A believer's prayer life is concerned with prayer fruit. Christians abide in the Vine. Receiving everything that a person could ever ask in prayer sounds outlandish. However, that is the way the Lord will work after a person receives the revelation of God's life flow in him or her. *You can ask anything in His name and it shall be done for you!*

> *Therefore you now have sorrow; but I will see you again and your heart will rejoice, and your joy no one will take from you. And in that day you will ask Me nothing. Most assuredly, I say to you, whatever you ask the Father in My name He will give you. Until now you have asked nothing in My name. Ask, and you will receive, that your joy may be full* (John 16:22-24).

GETTING ON TRACK

The agenda of angels is to get every Christian on track. Every believer who is on track will begin implementing the will of the Kingdom of God on this earth. Prayer life is where that implementation begins. Every believer's words are full of God's authority. A believer will walk in the holy fire of God wherever he or she goes if he or she walks in the authority of the Lord and completely trusts in the Lord. That fire will begin to spring forth from a devoted Christian and touch everything that he or she experiences. That holy fire comes from the holy altar of God at this very moment, and it is burning on and in every believer. Jesus is the One who baptizes Christians in the Spirit and in fire.

> *Those who repent I baptize with water, but there is coming a Man after me who is more powerful than I am. In fact, I'm not even worthy enough to pick up his sandals.* **He will submerge you into union with the Spirit of Holiness and with a raging fire!** (Matthew 3:11 TPT)

God desires that every Christian have complete joy. He is going to answer our prayers. The heavenly Father has given each believer the ability to act out His perfect will in life. Christians must lay hold of these truths and allow the Spirit of God to take them into this next step. They must be fully convinced of the will of God for their lives. Believers must recognize what Heaven wants to accomplish upon earth through them. There is nothing impossible to those who believe. There is a lot of fire in Heaven, and that fire is to be transferred to this earth.

Angels can handle their assignments and have the character to bring every believer through every battle to victory in Christ. Angels will not accept defeat in any way. Christians must develop a tenacity for victory that refuses to give up or let go until victory is reached. The angels are present to motivate Christians to implement the will of God for their lives and in this generation. The mission of angels contains a domino effect as they minister to people and influence this earthly environment with the environment of Heaven.

Therefore, since we are receiving a kingdom which cannot be shaken, let us have grace, by which we may serve God acceptably with reverence and godly fear. For our God is a consuming fire (Hebrews 12:28-29).

Chapter 12

THE ENEMIES OF ANGEL AGENDA

See, I am sending an angel before you to protect you on your journey and lead you safely to the place I have prepared for you. Pay close attention to him, and obey his instructions. Do not rebel against him, for he is my representative, and he will not forgive your rebellion.
—EXODUS 23:20-21 NLT

DISOBEDIENCE

Christians sometimes fail to recognize that angels can be grieved. A Christian can miss his or her divine appointment and fail, and then angels grieve. *Disobedience will not be tolerated.* Angels are very strict on certain issues with the people to whom they have been assigned. They are grieved when people do not act in humility toward the Lord and His will. The angels restart the process of discipline and training to bring a disobedient Christian into humbling himself or herself and entering into the rest of faith.

God gives angels commands and briefings that create an agenda for each angel. The source of the agenda for angels is the command center of Heaven. There, strategies concerning people's lives are discussed in detail. Destinies are discussed and determined based on what is already written in advance in the books about the person. Decisions are made concerning actions that may need to be taken. People cause these changes when they fail to obey or they do not grasp the will of God for their lives. Then, angels are sent to do certain missions. They are assigned for special purposes and special plans. These angels are similar to the special forces of the military.

> *For He shall give His angels charge over you, to keep you in all your ways. In their hands they shall bear you up, lest you dash your foot against a stone. You shall tread upon the lion and the cobra, the young lion and the serpent you shall trample underfoot* (Psalm 91:11-13).

There are all types of angels on different assignments, each having different qualities about them. A specific number of messenger angels help with communications. Some angels are scribes who just record conversations and events. "Then those who feared the Lord spoke to one another, and the Lord listened and heard them; so a book of remembrance was written before Him for those who fear the Lord and who meditate on His name" (Mal. 3:16). Others assist people to deliver messages. Archangels are on assignment against the bigger principalities and powers. There are enemies that pose a threat to *the agenda of angels*. Once a Christian understands these various types of angels and their assignments, he or she can effectively work with angels to implement the agenda of Heaven.

Christians must obey God. They must run full speed into this move of God, testifying about Jesus. The Lord wants Christians to tell everyone about the reconciliation that has taken place. All people must accept the sacrificial offering of Jesus, repent of their sins, and make Jesus the Lord of their lives. After every tongue, tribe, and nation has heard the Good News, believers will be translated into the new Kingdom age. The great catching away will happen. Just as Enoch was caught away, Christians will be caught up in the air. Believers will be walking with God, then they will suddenly disappear! They will be snatched away by God!

Christians will become irresistible to Father God. He will not be able to withstand being apart from His own anymore. He'll be so pleased by their faith that God will take them to be with Him. All the teachings in the Bible, including First Thessalonians, Second Thessalonians, Revelation, Daniel, and all the books of the prophets, focus upon this time at the end of the age when these things start to culminate. The sons of God are going to be revealed according to the apostle Paul.

DOUBT AND UNBELIEF

I was told to make sure the people know not to grieve their angels nor rebel against the work for the Lord. I do know that a Christian can provoke his angels by *doubt and unbelief.* According to the Book of Hebrews, this disobedience and unbelief was the very thing that happened in the desert when the Israelites did not enter into the rest. Here is what happened in the great exodus from Egypt:

See, I am sending an angel before you to protect you on your journey and lead you safely to the place I have prepared for you. Pay close attention to him, and obey his instructions. Do not rebel against him, for he is my representative, and he will not forgive your rebellion. But if you are careful to obey him, following all my instructions, then I will be an enemy to your enemies, and I will oppose those who oppose you. For my angel will go before you and bring you into the land of the Amorites, Hittites, Perizzites, Canaanites, Hivites, and Jebusites, so you may live there. And I will destroy them completely. You must not worship the gods of these nations or serve them in any way or imitate their evil practices. Instead, you must utterly destroy them and smash their sacred pillars. You must serve only the Lord your God. If you do, I will bless you with food and water, and I will protect you from illness. There will be no miscarriages or infertility in your land, and I will give you long, full lives. I will send my terror ahead of you and create panic among all the people whose lands you invade. I will make all your enemies turn and run (Exodus 23:20-27 NLT).

Angels will always fight God's enemies. They will take care of every Christian's enemies as well because believers are part of God's family. Angels also perceive that your enemies are their enemies. Just as the Lord did for the Israelites, as told in the verses above from Exodus, angels also create panic among the enemy when Christians invade the land of their enemies. The enemy will turn and run from believers in terror.

> ANGELS HAVE ALREADY LABELED YOUR ENEMIES
> AS THEIR ENEMIES BECAUSE GOD HAS TOLD THE
> ANGELS THAT HIS CHILDREN ARE IN COVENANT
> WITH THE HIM. SO NOW I AM HAS MADE YOU
> THE *AGENDA OF ANGELS*.

In this last day, it is of utmost importance that Christians honor the angels that the Lord has sent to assist them in fulfilling their destiny. Angels have been sent to fight for believers and to create panic among the enemies of believers. They are on missions that cause fear in every enemy to a believer. Angels cause those enemies to turn and run. Christians cannot be rebellious or in unbelief and they must respect the fact that God has placed angels into their lives to drive out the enemy before them.

REBELLION

The people of God did not enter into the rest because of their *unbelief! That unbelief was considered rebellion.* Angels absolutely do not want any Christian to be in rebellion. Angels want every Christian to yield to God's will for his or her life. Even if a Christian does not think he or she understands the reason for God's will for his or her life, there must be no rebellion. Believers must be humble and therefore be willing to ask for help. The Lord and His angels want every believer to verbally affirm that he or she is willing to submit to the will of God. A Christian must have the desire to do God's will and let God know it is a delight to do that will. Christians must humbly ask the Lord to reveal His will for their lives to them. Angels are working with Christians. Angels have a plan and purpose in God. Our heavenly Father is the Commander of the Lord's army, so believers must not rebel. He is implementing His agenda for the ages. Believers are part of this as the *agenda of angels*.

> *"I'm calling to you, sons of Adam, yes, and to you daughters as well. Listen to me and you will be prudent and wise. For even the foolish and feeble can receive an understanding heart that will change their inner being. The meaning of my words will release within you revelation for you to reign in life. My lyrics will empower you to live by what is right. For everything I say is unquestionably true, and I refuse to endure the lies of lawlessness—my words will never lead you astray. All the declarations of my mouth can be trusted; they contain no twisted logic or perversion of the truth. All my words are clear and straightforward to everyone who possesses spiritual understanding. If you have an open mind, you will receive revelation-knowledge. My wise correction is more valuable than silver or gold. The finest gold is nothing compared to the revelation-knowledge*

I can impart." Wisdom is so priceless that it exceeds the value of any jewel. Nothing you could wish for can equal her. "For I am Wisdom, and I am shrewd and intelligent. I have at my disposal living-understanding to devise a plan for your life. Wisdom pours into you when you begin to hate every form of evil in your life, for that's what worship and fearing God is all about. Then you will discover that your pompous pride and perverse speech are the very ways of wickedness that I hate! You will find true success when you find me, for I have insight into wise plans that are designed just for you. I hold in my hands living-understanding, courage, and strength. They're all ready and waiting for you. I empower kings to reign and rulers to make laws that are just. I empower princes to rise and take dominion, and generous ones to govern the earth. I will show my love to those who passionately love me. For they will search and search continually until they find me. Unending wealth and glory come to those who discover where I dwell. The riches of righteousness and a long, satisfying life will be given to them. What I impart has greater worth than gold and treasure, and the increase I bring benefits more than a windfall of income. I lead you into the ways of righteousness to discover the paths of true justice. Those who love me gain great wealth and a glorious inheritance, and I will fill their lives with treasures" (Proverbs 8:4-21 TPT).

God speaks only truth. If Christians will adhere to the promises in these verses, wisdom from Heaven will help them. They must allow Jesus Christ to rule in their lives. Here is a briefing and checklist for constant meditation to combat against *the enemies of angel agenda.*

SECRET WISDOM BRIEFING CHECKLIST

1. **Listen to me and you will be prudent and wise.**

    - For even the foolish and feeble can receive an understanding heart. That will change their inner being.

2. **The meaning of my words will release within you revelation.**

    - For you to reign in life.

3. **My lyrics will empower you to live by what is right.**

    - For everything I say is unquestionably true.
    - I refuse to endure the lies of lawlessness.
    - My words will never lead you astray.

4. **All the declarations of my mouth can be trusted.**

    - They contain no twisted logic or perversion of the truth.

5. **All my words are clear and straightforward to everyone.**

    - One must possess spiritual understanding.

6. **If one has an open mind, one will receive revelation-knowledge.**

7. **My wise correction is more valuable than silver or gold.**

    - The finest gold is nothing compared to the revelation-knowledge I can impart.

8. **Wisdom is so priceless that it exceeds the value of any jewel.**

    - Nothing you could wish for can equal her.

9. **I am Wisdom, and I am shrewd and intelligent.**

10. **I have at my disposal living-understanding.**

    - To devise a plan for every believer's life.

11. **Wisdom pours into each believer.**

    - When you begin to hate every form of evil in your life.

    - For that is the crux of worship and fearing God.

12. **You will discover what I think of their pompous pride and perverse speech.**

    - They are the very ways of wickedness that I hate!

13. **You will find true success when you find me.**

    - For I have insight into wise plans that are designed just for you.

14. **I hold in my hands living-understanding, courage, and strength.**

    - They're all ready and waiting for you.

15. **I empower kings to reign and rulers to make laws that are just.**

16. **I empower princes to rise and take dominion, and generous ones to govern the earth.**

17. **I will show my love to those who passionately love me.**

    - For they will search and search continually until they find me.

18. **Unending wealth and glory come to those who discover where I dwell.**

19. **The riches of righteousness and a long, satisfying life will be given to them.**

20. **What I impart has greater worth than gold and treasure.**

    - There is increase; I bring benefits more than a windfall of income.

21. **I lead you into the ways of righteousness.**

    - You will discover the paths of true justice.

22. **Those who love me gain great wealth and a glorious inheritance.**

    - I will fill their lives with treasures.

> REALIZE TODAY THE LORD HAS SENT YOU AMAZ-
> ING ANGELS WHO PERFORM VERY POWERFUL
> SERVICE IN ORDER TO HELP YOU WALK IN THE
> WILL OF GOD.

Wisdom should govern the lives of every believer. Rebellion should not exist in any Christian because God hates it. He hates wickedness, perverse speech, and pride. Wisdom drives out pride from a person's life. A person who allows humility to rule will not be hindered. Angels do not like to deal with prideful people. Angels enjoy dealing to with those who have a servant's heart. People who are humble and broken know that they need God. Humble people understand *repentance* and the *altar of God*. They understand *waiting on God*, the *fear of the Lord*, and *deep spiritual worship*.

UNHEALED SOUL WOUNDS

One thing that I was briefed upon when I met with Jesus concerned wounds in the souls of leadership in the church. Healing must flow to all those who have been traumatically attacked by satan. The Lord revealed that the move of the Holy Spirit is on the earth right now. He also said that at this present time, the glory of the Father is revealed. I saw that leaders were not retaining the glory. It was leaking through holes in their souls. The glory would come forth in a meeting, but the move of God could not be sustained. Leadership has been attacked. Leadership must pray and deal with failure to forgive. The Holy Spirit wants to minister the love of Father God to those leaders who have been offended so that offense is driven out.

This includes every Christian as well who must allow the Holy Spirit to do His work to heal any wounds they may have endured. Believers must drive out any failure to forgive because it can hinder the work of the Lord. They must forgive right now and let it go.

MERCHANDISING THE GLORY

The glory of God, which was the Ark of the Covenant in the Old Testament, was to be on poles. These poles were to be in place, according to the instructions given by God to Moses on the mountain. No one was allowed to touch the Ark of the Covenant. They were to carry it with poles. Only the special Levitical priests and the high priest were allowed to be around the Ark. At the end time, the Ark of the Covenant, which represented the presence of God and the glory of God, must be carried correctly and not put on display as merchandise. God showed me the Ark on a cart instead of being carried on poles. When the Ark is pictured as being upon the cart instead of being carried in this manner, it symbolizes a grave error—the move of the glory of the Father is being merchandised. This merchandizing is an enemy of the move of God in the glory. Angels are grieved when this happens. No Christian should allow the glory of God to be displayed on a cart to be merchandised. The glory of God is not for spectators. God does not reveal Himself for spectators. He reveals His glory for the sons and daughters of the Kingdom, who are participants in the glory of God.

ANGELS ARE IMPLEMENTING THE WILL OF GOD

FOR YOUR LIFE. YOU JUST NEED TO LET GO OF

ALL THE TRAUMATIC EVENTS AND ANYTHING THAT HAS OCCURRED FROM PEOPLE WHO HAVE HURT YOU. JUST HAND OVER THOSE CASE FILES TO THE LORD. LET HIM TAKE THE CASE AND SETTLE WITH THE COURTS OF HEAVEN. DO NOT ALLOW OFFENSE TO ROB YOU OF THE JOY OF THE LORD.

CONCLUSION

No one knows the spirit realm better than the Holy Spirit. He is the Master of His own realm. Through Jesus Christ, the Holy Spirit will give every Christian entrance into His domain. He gives to every believer eyes that see and ears that hear. He is developing everyone's spirit. He is making certain that every believer is rejecting pride through the gift of repentance. This repentance comes at the *holy altar of God*. God, by His Spirit, is allowing humility and brokenness to come when each believer submits his or her will completely to God.

When the Lord gives Christians everything that He has in His treasuries, He wins hearts. As this happens, Christians learn to hate what God hates and to love what God loves. The apostle Peter gave us a very good understanding of what God has done for us through Jesus Christ:

> *May grace and perfect peace cascade over you as you live in the rich knowledge of God and of Jesus our*

Lord. Everything we could ever need for life and complete devotion to God has already been deposited in us by his divine power. For all this was lavished upon us through the rich experience of knowing him who has called us by name and invited us to come to him through a glorious manifestation of his goodness. As a result of this, he has given you magnificent promises that are beyond all price, so that through the power of these tremendous promises you can experience partnership with the divine nature, by which you have escaped the corrupt desires that are of the world. So devote yourselves to lavishly supplementing your faith with goodness, and to goodness add understanding, and to understanding add the strength of self-control, and to self-control add patient endurance, and to patient endurance add godliness, and to godliness add mercy toward your brothers and sisters, and to mercy toward others add unending love. Since these virtues are already planted deep within, and you possess them in abundant supply, they will keep you from being inactive or fruitless in your pursuit of knowing Jesus Christ more intimately. But if anyone lacks these things, he is blind, constantly closing his eyes to the mysteries of our faith, and forgetting his innocence—for his past sins have been washed away. For this reason, beloved ones, be eager to confirm and validate that God has invited you to salvation and claimed you as his own. If you do these things, you will never stumble. As a result, the kingdom's gates will open wide to you as God choreographs your

*triumphant entrance into the eternal kingdom of our
Lord and Savior, Jesus the Messiah* (2 Peter 1:2-11
TPT).

God's angels want the best for God's own. Angels are empowered by the Word of God and the will of God. They assist so many people in so many different generations. They have been around much longer than human beings. Christians can shine in this last day with angels' assistance. *The agenda of angels* is to help Christians realize that God is preparing people's hearts for what is occurring on the earth at present. God desires for every believer to comprehend how much He loves this generation. He wants this generation of believers to come back to their first love. The Holy Spirit wants to remind people that it is not just about the life that they live, but about the *agenda of God*. The agenda of Heaven should be matching up with the *agenda of the church* and the believers who compose the church. *The agenda of angels* brings Christians into the heart and intention of Father God. In times of prayer, believers may find themselves attending the same briefing room in the *command center of Heaven* with the same angels who have so faithfully watched over them.

See you there!

ABOUT DR. KEVIN ZADAI

Kevin Zadai, Th.D. was called to ministry at the age of ten. He attended Central Bible College in Springfield, Missouri, where he received a Bachelor of Arts in theology. Later, he received training in missions at Rhema Bible College. He is currently ordained through Rev. Dr. Jesse and Rev. Dr. Cathy Duplantis. At age thirty-one, during a routine day surgery, he found himself on the "other side of the veil" with Jesus. For forty-five minutes, the Master revealed spiritual truths before returning him to his body and assigning him to a supernatural ministry. Kevin holds a commercial pilot license and is retired from Southwest Airlines after twenty-nine years as a flight attendant. He and his lovely wife, Kathi, reside in New Orleans, Louisiana.

OTHER BOOKS BY DR. KEVIN ZADAI

Heavenly Visitation

Heavenly Visitation Study Guide

Heavenly Visitation Prayer Guide

Days of Heaven on Earth

Days of Heaven on Earth Study Guide

Days of Heaven on Earth Prayer Guide

A Meeting Place with God

Your Hidden Destiny Revealed

Praying from the Heavenly Realms

SALVATION PRAYER

Lord God,

I confess that I am a sinner. I confess that I need Your Son, Jesus.

Please forgive me in His name.

Lord Jesus, I believe You died for me and that You are alive and listening to me now.

I now turn from my sins and welcome You into my heart.

Come and take control of my life. Make me the kind of person You want me to be.

Now, fill me with Your Holy Spirit who will show me how to live for You. I acknowledge You before men as my Savior and my Lord.

In Jesus's name. Amen.

If you prayed this prayer, please contact us at info@kevinzadai.com for more information and material. Go to KevinZadai.com for other exciting ministry materials.

Join our network
at
Warriornotes.tv

Join our ministry training school
at
Warriornotes School of Ministry

More info at
KevinZadai.com